# ALL
## ABOARD!

# ALL
## ABOARD!

TALES OF AUSTRALIAN RAILWAYS

JIM HAYNES & RUSSELL HANNAH

ABC
Books

Published by ABC Books for the
AUSTRALIAN BROADCASTING CORPORATION
GPO Box 9994 Sydney NSW 2001

*First published November 2004*
*Reprinted September 2009*

ISBN 978 0 7333 1499 5

*Front cover photograph by Dennis Forbes, courtesy of Eveleigh Press*
*Back cover photograph courtesy of NSW SA*
*Cover and internal design by Christabella Designs*
*Illustration by Lucy Pollard*
*Typeset by Kirby Jones in 12pt on 16pt Bembo*
*Colour reproduction by Colorwize, Adelaide*
*Printed and bound by Quality Printing, Hong Kong*
*5 4 3 2*

This book is dedicated to Lyle Hannah, who spent half a lifetime on the railways and always said: 'There are only two classes in society: those who worked on the railways and those who wished they did.'

# ABOUT THE AUTHORS

 Before becoming a professional entertainer in 1988, **Jim Haynes** taught in schools and universities from outback New South Wales to the UK and back again. He has two masters degrees in literature, from the University of New England and the University of Wales.

Winner of 'Comedy Song of the Year' four times at the Tamworth Country Music Festival, including the hits 'Don't Call Wagga Wagga Wagga' and 'Since Cheryl Went Feral', Jim has released many albums of his own songs, verse and humour.

He has won the Bush Laureate Book of the Year award three times – in 1996 for *I'll Have Chips*, in 2001 for the compilation *An Australian Heritage of Verse*, and again in 2004 for *An Australian Treasury of Popular Verse*.

 **Russell Hannah**'s earliest memory is travelling to Sydney from Murwillumbah on the North Coast Mail. His father had taken a job on the railways and was bringing the family to Sydney to live. He has loved trains ever since.

Having taught for forty years in schools, prisons, mental institutions and TAFE colleges without ever working out which was which, Russell is now retired. He lives in Shellharbour with his wife Bev. They have three grown-up children.

Russell has been involved in the folk movement for many years and is president of the Illawarra Folk Club, as well as convenor of the South Coast Tripe Eating Association. He has a degree in micropaleontology (which he can no longer spell) and enjoys an occasional drink with his mates Leo the Lover, Henry the Hun and Backhoe Bill.

# ACKNOWLEDGMENTS

Our special thanks go to Grahame Watt; Wilbur Howcroft; Dawn Burchill; David and Bobbie Field; Chris Holley; Bob Gallagher at Eveleigh Press; Ken Williams at the Australian Railways Historical Society NSW Railway Resource Centre; Russell 'Rusty' Bright; Nick Lewicki, Secretary of the Public Transport Union; Andrew West, Librarian Queensland Division Australian Railways Historical Society; Paddy and Debbie Hodglein at the Railway Junction Hotel, Wolumla; Ken Scarlett, Brian Dunnett, Simon Hurford, Chris Cartledge, Nick Erby and Daryll Griffiths; the family of the late Ray Nicholls; Terry Martin at Thirlmere Rail and Tram Museum; Brigitta Doyle for the guidance, Sally Cohen for the typing, Jon Gibbs for the quality control, Stuart Neal and ABC Books; the Mitchell Library.

For their assistance with stories we would like to thank Bob Brain and Chris Holley for their personal memories; Peter Kitcher from the Rail Motor Society for his help on Tin Hares; Peter Sexton for the breakfast story; Maurie Mulheron and Fred Moore for the Fair-go McDonald story; Ray Laneryie for his story on late trains; Alex and Annette Hood for the Timetable Scottie story; Ted Egan for information on the Ghan; Dave Chessor for the ice story; those great characters, Leo the Lover, Henry the Hun and Backhoe Bill.

For their assistance with photographs, we thank Russell 'Rusty' Bright; John Elliott; David and Bobbie Field; Dennis Forbes; Bob Gallagher; Chris Holley; Ken Williams; Kerry Otten and Kerry

Alexander at Wollongong City Library; Deirdre at the Noel Butlin Archives Centre ANU; Koulla Giannikouris and Linda Marchesani at Northern Territory Library; Judith Jensen at Thuringowa City Library; Norm Ricaud and Emily Hanna at NSW State Archives; Australian Railways Historical Society NSW Railway Resource Centre; Brisbane City Council; Eveleigh Press; New South Wales State Archive; New South Wales Public Transport Union; Northern Territory Library; Noel Butlin Archives Centre, Australian National University; Thuringowa City Library; Werris Creek Rail Town Museum; Wollongong City Library and Illawarra Historical Society.

# CONTENTS

# INTRODUCTION

*All Aboard! Tales of Australian Railways* is a collection of Australian railway stories. They were chosen, first and foremost, for their value as stories, their entertainment value. We were also very keen to find or write stories that dealt with some element of the history, characters and culture of the Australian railways. So these stories have one thing in common: the railway is in some way central to each one.

The year 2004 marks the 150th anniversary of the railway in Australia, and the railways were the largest employers in Australia for over a hundred of those years. There are very few Australians who do not have at least one relative or ancestor that worked on the railways in some capacity.

Some stories in this collection are drawn from the lives of the workers – the railway pioneers who opened up the outback, the navvies who laid the rails, the men and women who drove the trains, sorted the freight and fed the passengers. Some stories are very real. Historic figures like John Whitton and Ben Chifley feature in true accounts of their lives and achievements. Other stories are also accurate memoirs of real people, like Chris Holley, who spent his working life with the railway, and Bob Brain, who was one of the many injured in the 1977 Granville Disaster.

Then there are stories about genuine, but larger-than-life, railway characters. Colourful figures like Stargazer Jones who worked all their lives on the railways and about whom so many tales are told that it's hard to tell fact from fiction. These sorts of stories were mostly

Staff at Eveleigh Workshops, Sydney, 1920. 'For 100 years the railways would remain the largest single source of employment in Australia.' ANU NB

collected as anecdotes from old railway workers like Russell's dad, Lyle Hannah, and from various government and union archives.

We have also invented characters of our own in order to tell some of the stories we collected, and to prevent legal action being taken against us. (We fear, however, that some of Russell's drinking companions may recognise themselves rather easily; they have promised not to sue.) Leo the Lover and his mates, Henry the Hun and Backhoe Bill and the others, are, we maintain, fictional characters who just happen to enjoy a good yarn and reminisce often about the railways. We hope readers enjoy sitting in on their conversations.

Of course, no collection of railway stories would be complete without accounts of railway journeys, both memorable and forgettable. There have been some very notable passengers on Australia's railways. Some of these illustrious figures, like Mark Twain, D.H. Lawrence and Robert Louis Stevenson, wrote specifically about our railways or used them as the backdrop for their own stories.

Although this book is not a history of the railways in any shape or form, there are some pieces that deal with the history and politics of

Australia's railways, tales of farce and failure, tragedy and drama, as well as stories of expansion, development and success.

It was on 2 August 1854 that Australia's first train journey took place. On that day the first train puffed its way out of Melbourne Station (now Flinders Street Station) on the short run to Port Melbourne. It was a gala occasion and an important first for Melbourne – one in the eye for rival city Sydney.

When the train reached the astonishing maximum speed of 24 kilometres an hour, a reporter onboard noted that 'at that speed the countryside became a blur!' Few among the thousands waving and cheering that day would have realised the effect the railway would have on our growing nation over the next century or so.

Australia's development coincided exactly with the development of rail transport, and for a hundred years the railways would remain the largest single source of employment in Australia. Large towns grew up because of the railways, and thousands of smaller settlements owed their entire existence to them. Even before the trains ran, townships developed around the navvy camps, with shops and pubs and workshops. These navvies helped the country grow in more ways than one – the local population often increased after the workers went through. The railways also provided an impetus for immigration and work for the thousands of men who rushed to Australia looking for gold.

The early navvies were pioneers in many cases. They laid the rails across the plains and mountains and into the outback, and they conquered different kinds of landscapes with hard, physical work. They sweated and toiled long hours in dangerous places, lived in harsh conditions and suffered the extremes of heat and cold. They were often the first Europeans to stay more than a few days or weeks in many remote areas.

A number of navvies perished as they opened up the inland. Getting the railway across the Great Divide was particularly tricky and fraught with danger, while over thirty navvies died building less than 30 miles of the track from Cairns to Kuranda in northern Queensland.

Once the Great Zig Zag was completed across the Great Dividing Range west of Sydney in 1869, the coast and the city were linked forever to the bush. Passengers and freight could travel easily from Bourke to Sydney. In fact the railway grew so quickly after the Zig Zag was finished that the rails reached the bush towns years before they reached most suburbs of Sydney. The railway arrived in Bourke before it arrived in Hurstville!

As well as freight and passengers, the railway kept people all over Australia in touch with each other as never before, because it also carried *the mail*. On many outback railway runs, the mail was actually sorted as the train steamed west – the train was truly a travelling post office.

The railways changed every facet of life in Australia. They altered the face of cities and suburbs forever, but the impact the railways had in opening up the bush and the outback is immeasurable. Even the advent of those Aussie icons the drovers was in a sense a result of the railways. The great droving tracks ended at rail heads like Dajarra and Maree, so naturally that's where the drovers were always headed with their mobs of cattle. Australia's great cattle drives were a result of the railway being available at the end of the journey.

Railways meant relatively easy access from the cities to the outback, and from city to city. Thus, Australia's population was mobile as never before. If you were restless or unhappy, well, you could take a train to somewhere else …

There were many ways to travel with the railways. During the Great Depression of the 1930s, men had to move a certain distance to get rations. The idea was that they were looking for work – of course, there really wasn't any work and many men tried to get around the countryside by taking a free ride on a goods train. If they were caught they were locked up in the local nick and forced to chop wood and do other hard labour for their tucker. Unfortunately, there were many uncomfortable train trips, whether you rode in the carriage or in a freight car. But with the decline of the railways during the 1970s, those of us who loved the railway began to experience a far worse fate: when the trains were taken off the rails, they were replaced by buses on the roads.

The railways took Australians into the bush and brought the bush into the cities. The railways employed vast numbers of Aussies, stimulated immigration and population growth, made rural development and primary industry viable, and provided us with some of the most farcical and fascinating chapters in our nation's history.

Today we see a growth in railways for the first time in many decades. The permanent way is making a comeback and the divisions of the different track gauges have almost been conquered. We will never see rail return to the heady days of the late nineteenth and early twentieth centuries when trains were the most used form of transport in the country, but it seems that trains will be with us for a long time yet.

The stories here in *All Aboard! Tales of Australian Railways* are an attempt to recapture something of those past glory days of the railways. They are just a small sample of the fiction, anecdotes, history, myths and legends that the railways of Australia have inspired over the years. They are told with as much loving care as we can muster, as a tribute to those who worked on the Australian railways and gave them their unique Aussie character.

'Australia's population was mobile as never before.' NSW SA

# THIN ICE

▼▼▼▼▼▼▼▼▼▼▼▼▼▼▼▼▼▼▼▼▼▼▼▼▼▼▼▼▼▼▼▼▼▼▼▼▼▼▼▼▼▼▼▼▼▼▼▼▼▼▼▼▼

*by Russell Hannah & Jim Haynes*

I was having a quiet drink with Leo the Lover. Leo is an old railwayman, erstwhile railway historian and local identity who drinks at my club. In fact, he is something of a storyteller-in-residence at the club.

As his name implies, Leo the Lover has at least one strong suit. Although his strong suit may not be truthfulness, most of Leo's stories have some sort of factual basis.

We were sitting under the TV set in the bar. Leo the Lover always sits under the TV set. If there is one thing Leo can't abide it's a TV set blaring away when he is having a quiet ale. You see, Leo is a talker and he finds that television interrupts his train of thought when he's telling a tale.

So, why does Leo sit under the TV set? Well, if anyone wants to turn it up, they have to get past Leo, so mostly they deem it more judicious to pop into the lounge bar to watch the TV in there.

'It's your shout,' said a voice from behind me. 'Mine's a whisky and soda – no ice.'

I looked around and there was Leo's old drinking mate and sparring partner, Henry the Hun. It always seems to be my shout when Henry arrives, but I never complain. Henry's pretty good on the gab himself and has led a very varied life. He has many stories to tell also, and if there's one thing I love, it's a good yarn.

Henry's known as Henry the Hun because of his surname. Even though his family have been in Australia for four generations, Henry's Germanic surname is one that most people can't pronounce, so most of his mates just call him 'the Hun'.

I must say, Henry takes this in good spirit and rarely shows any aggravation. I occasionally suspect that he has difficulty with his name himself. I caught him looking at his driver's licence one day when he needed to sign a cheque.

Now, I've bought Henry whisky many times before and no matter how hot the day, Henry always adds the 'no ice' rider to his order.

'You must have a bit of Pom in you,' I said to him as I returned with the whisky. 'Only a Pom would like his drinks warm on such a hot day.'

'I'll tell you a true story,' said Henry. 'It'll give you an understanding of why I have such an aversion to ice.

'Many years ago, in my youth, I was a painter for the Public Works Department, and one of our jobs was to travel the state painting small bush schools. We worked in gangs of two and, in general, it was a good job. The pay wasn't great but we received a pretty good "living away from home" allowance, most of which we were able to save, as the headmaster would generally let us camp in the weather shed. Of course, we got to see the inside of many country pubs, where we happily contributed our living expenses to the Publican's Retirement Fund.

'Now, one time we had to paint the school at a little place called Bardalungra. Bardalungra consisted of a few houses, a pub, a garage and general store combined and the obligatory one-teacher school. Bardalungra was a place destined for oblivion.

'There was, of course, one more building, and that was the railway station. The station was small. A weatherboard waiting room attached to a signal box that contained all those mysterious levers that enable trains to pass when there's a single line. Not that trains ever passed much at Bardalungra. It was a branch line that was serviced by a "mixed" – a goods train with a passenger carriage attached. The carriage was for those travellers who either had plenty of time for their journey or, like us, had a government rail warrant.

Mixed trains on branch lines carried a surprising variety of goods. NSW SA

'The old trundler was not noted for speed. It was also one of those trains that, for reasons I could never understand, would stop at irregular intervals. It would stop at sidings that barely existed, or even in what seemed to be open paddocks, and just stay there for a while.

'The train only ran four times a week, except in harvest time, when a few trains were used to cart barley and wheat. That was the only time there was any other traffic on the line.

'Well, my mate and myself caught the train to Bardalungra one stinking hot day. It was one of those days when you dream of swimming pools and cold beer. The only "air-conditioning" available was to open the windows, but the air outside was hotter than inside: that dry heat of summer in western New South Wales.

'The irony of it all was that we had six bottles of beer with us that we'd bought the night before at a pub in Moree. We'd bought a dozen and for some reason still had six left when we finally hit the sack. Unfortunately, they were at least as hot as the air in the carriage, so we'd put off drinking them till we could find some suitable refrigeration.

'Not surprisingly, we were the only people in the carriage. We soon struck up a conversation with the guard, as you always did on country trains back then. He was a large friendly character with a florid face, the kind of bloke who looked like he might like a cold drink on a hot day, or any other day for that matter. He soon left the guard's van and joined us. It seemed he liked a bit of company – there being very few people travelling on the line – and it wasn't long before he knew all there was to know about us and we knew all about him.

'It also wasn't long before he noticed our six large bottles of beer sitting on the seat. "I see you boys have got a bit of the good liquid refreshment there," he said. "Are you going teetotal today?"

'Now, our throats were pretty dry and our heads were a bit heavy from the previous night. We explained that, as much as we'd love a beer, we couldn't bring ourselves to drink beer that was quite so hot.

'"I can fix you up, lads," he said. "I've got some ice in the van – next stop I'll pop back and bring some up."

'The guard's van was separated from our carriage by several goods wagons and, as luck would have it, the next stop wasn't far away. He soon disappeared back to his van and returned with a billy can half full of ice. Before too long we had the water glasses down from the carriage

Branch-line trains often stopped at sidings like these for no apparent reason. NSW SA

wall and were happily into our first bottle of cold beer. Naturally, the guard joined us. After all, it was a hot day.

'It seemed that our new mate the guard had an endless supply of ice. At every stop he'd go back to his van and return with more ice in the billy. He wasn't a bad drinker either. He certainly managed to put away his fair share of our beer.

'After a while we were on our last bottle and feeling quite affectionate towards our new mate, the railways, and the world in general. We were also regretting that we didn't have another six bottles left over from the night before. When we expressed this opinion to the guard, he remarked that it was probably a good thing – as he was about to run out of ice.

'Perhaps it was about then that I really began to wonder where this seemingly endless supply of ice had come from. It didn't take long to find out.

'The train soon made another of its interminable stops, at a small siding which had a name that thankfully I forget. The guard had left us to do "a bit of work" in his van.

'As I leaned idly out the window, my belly full of cold beer, I noticed a black panel van and two well-dressed blokes standing by the siding. That's funny, I thought to myself. That van looks like a *hearse*. I soon realised what "bit of work" the guard had returned to his van to do. As I watched, the doors of the guard's van opened. Then, the two well-dressed blokes and the guard lifted a coffin out of the train and into the back of the black panel van.

'It was then,' said Henry the Hun, finishing his scotch, 'that I knew where the ice had come from.'

'Henry,' I told him, 'that story was almost plausible. I'm beginning to think that some of your yarns have an element of truth in them.'

'That's the only time you've ever been right about anything,' said Henry. 'It's your shout again – I'll have a beer this time. And, by the way,' he chuckled, 'no ice ...'

# FROM ENGINE DRIVER TO PRIME MINISTER

*by Russell Hannah*

My dad knew Ben Chifley. That in itself is not strange. My father was a train driver, and so was Ben Chifley. But then almost every old engine man I ever met claimed to have known Ben Chifley. I have even known railwaymen who were born after Ben died who claimed to have known him.

I have never challenged these assertions. I never challenge people who claim to have met God, or ghosts or angels either, so why would I challenge anyone who claimed to have met the greatest engine driver this country ever produced? After all, Ben Chifley was like a god to most railwaymen.

I grew up in a house where politics was rarely discussed; we were working class, conservative and voted Labor. I instinctively knew this, even though when I asked my mother how she voted, she always said that it was a secret ballot and you didn't tell anyone.

Voting day and polling places were as mysterious as the corner pub, and to be able to enter them was a sign of being grown up. When I grew up and sampled the pleasures of both, I found the corner pub a little more appealing.

Bob Menzies presided over the country and looked a bit like our Sunday school version of God, with his white hair, commanding presence

Ben Chifley's Bathurst home is now a museum. RH

and bushy eyebrows. It wasn't until I grew up that I realised how fallible he was. We might have been a Labor household but, in our house, my mother (and therefore everyone else) always referred to Menzies as 'Mr Menzies'. Chifley, however, was always 'Ben Chifley', or just plain 'Ben'.

'Ben Chifley,' said my father, 'was the greatest prime minister Australia has ever had.' Who was I to argue? As a kid I believed everything my parents told me. I grew up holding the beliefs that I picked up in that little fibro house in the outer suburbs of Sydney. I shed many of those moral, political and religious beliefs at an early age but, somehow, I never did shed my belief in Ben Chifley. Even the events that brought about his electoral defeat – his attempts to nationalise the banks, one of the last great jousts of the labour movement against entrenched power – seemed heroic to me.

Ben Chifley was a railwayman. He was born in 1885 at Bathurst and remained there all his life. As prime minister he always stayed at the Kurrajong Hotel in Canberra – no Lodge or Kirribilli House for him. He returned to his modest cottage near Bathurst Railway Station whenever he could.

Chifley joined the railways in 1903 as a shop boy and quickly made his way through the very rigid hierarchy of the day. He rose through the ranks of cleaner, acting fireman, fireman, acting driver and was finally promoted to driver in 1914. This was no mean achievement for a man who had only an elementary schooling, though he had studied extensively at night with the Workers Educational Association. Chifley was active in the Railways Union and was one of its leaders in Bathurst. He was also an instructor in the training schools for firemen and drivers, often teaching men much older than himself.

In 1917, just three years after he became a driver, one of the most bitter strikes in Australia's history occurred. It lasted for over five weeks and split the Railways Union. The government brought in strikebreakers to attempt to run a skeleton service, recruiting farmers from country areas, students from Sydney University and even schoolboys from some of the private schools like King's and Sydney Grammar School.

There were many railway workers who didn't strike and others who trickled back to work during the dispute. The ensuing bitterness lasted

How many King's School boys did it take to do a railway cleaner's job in the 1917 strike? Eighteen plus supervisors. NSW SA

for decades, with the strikebreakers being known as the Loyalists, and the strikers, the Lilywhites.

Two weeks into the strike the government sacked all the strikers and deregistered their unions, declaring that they would not deal with the union leaders. The dispute was eventually settled in the government's favour. The unions firmly believed that, as part of the agreement, the sacked men would be re-employed and the government would not act vindictively against the strikers. However, the commissioner for Railways, James Fraser, had drawn up a list of 3000 men who were not to be re-employed.

Bathurst railway depot had been a hundred per cent solid during the strike, so in retrospect it was no surprise that one of those on the list was Joseph Benedict Chifley. When he reapplied for his job Chifley was advised that his services were no longer required. It took an appeal for Chifley to be reinstated but he lost his seniority and privileges. His pay was cut and he was demoted to the rank of fireman/acting driver. It was a great indignity for Chifley and the other Lilywhites. For many years after, they had to fire the engines for drivers who had scabbed during the strike.

Ben Chifley, engine driver and prime minister. NSW SA

They say it's an ill wind that blows no good and, in Chifley's case, that strike and its results stirred his strong sense of justice and fair play and pushed him into a political career. He later said in Parliament:

*I should not be a member of this parliament today if some tolerance had been extended to the men who took part in the strike of 1917. All that that harsh and oppressive treatment did as far as I was concerned was to transform me, with the assistance of my colleagues, from an ordinary engine driver into the Prime Minister of this country.*

My father remembers clearly a railways recruiting billboard near Redfern Station that read: 'A Cleaner Today, A Driver Tomorrow.' Underneath a graffiti-writer had added: 'And the Prime Minister the Day After!'

Some idea of the bitterness and recriminations over the strike of 1917 can be seen by the fact that when Jack Lang's Labor government was elected in 1925, one of its first acts was to restore the rights and privileges of the 1917 strikers. In 1928 the election of the Bavin Conservative government saw those rights again stripped from the 1917 Lilywhites. It was only in 1931, fourteen years after the great strike, with Lang again in power, that the rights were finally restored permanently.

The bad feeling between railwaymen at the workface lived on. An irreconcilable schism existed between the Lilywhites and the Loyalists. Keith Scarlett, who joined the railways in 1945, recalls how at Lithgow, where he was stationed, drivers would lean out of their engine cabins and yell 'You scabby old bastard!' at a stationmaster who hadn't joined the strike in 1917.

My father, Lyle Hannah, came down from the country and joined the railways in 1948. As a fireman, he was teamed up with the railways' most senior driver, Ernie Dews. Ernie had been a Lilywhite in 1917 and had lost both his job and privileges, so his bitterness for those who didn't strike had lived on. One day, when they were taking a train over the Blue Mountains and had pulled into Wentworth Falls Station, Ernie looked out and saw the guard from their train standing on the platform. He immediately recognised the guard as a 1917 Loyalist, a non-striker.

'Well, just look at that, Lyle,' said Ernie. 'That bastard scabbed in 1917 and now he's riding in our guard's van. Bugger him! Let's leave him on the platform.'

And that was exactly what they did. They steamed off, leaving the guard stranded on Wentworth Falls Station. The stationmaster had to get authority to hire a taxi to send him to Katoomba to pick the train up again. Of course, it was against regulations to leave guards on platforms, and the inevitable disciplinary action ensued. My dad said, 'Ernie got fined five shillings and I got fined two and sixpence – but Ernie reckoned it was worth it.'

Ben Chifley would have agreed. His reaction to his unfair dismissal was certainly worth it from the nation's point of view. He went on to guide Australia through the final year of World War II and his government paved the way for the nation's postwar expansion with much-needed social reforms and immigration initiatives.

In 1951 Ben Chifley died in Canberra in his room at the Kurrajong Hotel, but he wasn't buried in Canberra. He was brought back to Bathurst for his funeral and it's still the biggest ever to be held in that town. Ten years later his widow, Elizabeth, died, after which his cottage near the railway became a museum. Locomotive 5112, one that Ben drove, is also restored as a museum piece in his beloved Bathurst.

And how did my father know Ben Chifley? Well, in the last years of his life, when Parliament wasn't sitting, Ben would often return to his little cottage at 10 Busby Street, Bathurst. There he would sit on the porch, pipe in hand, and railwaymen would come to chat and pay homage to the nation's most famous engine driver. If my dad and Ernie Dews had time off in Bathurst they'd stroll up Busby Street and, if Ben was there, they'd stop by.

What did they chat about? Affairs of state? The international situation? Politics? No. Steam trains and railwaymen, of course.

# WHAT'S IN A NAME?

*by Russell Hannah*

The railway station serving the South Coast town of Shellharbour is known these days as 'Dunmore (Shellharbour)'. This has not always been the case, however; it was originally known simply as Shellharbour despite the fact that it is situated in the hamlet of Dunmore. Dunmore is made up of a dozen or so cottages that struggle up one side of Shellharbour Road, with a rural fire station tucked in between them. Dunmore's chief claim to fame is that all the houses in the village back onto the municipal tip.

On the other hand, the much more substantial 'village' of Shellharbour, situated 4 kilometres up the road and well out of sight of the station, is a thriving township and tourist resort. It has a pub, several clubs (including the one where Leo the Lover holds court), restaurants, al fresco dining establishments, takeaways, schools and shops, and it attracts many tourists and travellers of all kinds.

This is the story of how the name change from 'Shellharbour' to 'Dunmore (Shellharbour)' supposedly came about. It concerns David Hill, one-time general manager of the ABC and for a time chief executive of NSW State Rail.

One day David Hill had a strange notion for a state government chief executive officer: he decided it would be beneficial to his understanding of his job if he actually went out and experienced the joys of train travel from the point of view of an ordinary paying

17

Confusion over station names was not confined to Shellharbour. RH

passenger. So, rather than travelling well-heralded in the pampered luxury of the commissioner's special car, he would, once a month or so, select a destination from the list of stations and travel incognito, making notes and checking on staff, service and comfort as he went.

Inevitably, one day his selection was Shellharbour and, thinking this would be a pleasant trip to a seaside resort, he boarded the train at Sydney's Central Station and enjoyed the scenic trip down the coast.

When he reached Shellharbour Station, however, he alighted from the train and found himself surrounded by cow paddocks. Now, David Hill was no dill. He noticed the straggle of houses on the other side of the road but realised immediately that this couldn't possibly be the famous seaside resort town of Shellharbour, even though the station signs were telling him so. After all, he couldn't even see the sea.

This was back in the days when the railways actually employed a few people to man even the smaller stations. Sure enough, there, clad in an ill-fitting uniform and waiting to collect Hill's ticket was a sixteen-year-old junior station assistant.

Before ... <small>NSW SA</small>

After ... <small>RH</small>

'Well,' said David Hill to the kid, 'this clearly isn't Shellharbour township.'

'No mate,' replied the kid, who had no idea who he was talking to. 'This is Dunmore.'

'Ahh, I see,' said Hill. 'Well, where's Shellharbour?'

The kid pointed up the Shellharbour Road and said, 'It's up the road there a bit, just over the hill — it's about four kilometres away.'

'That's a bit strange, isn't it?' mused the boss of the railways. 'Wouldn't you think that they'd have built the station a bit closer to the town than this? Shellharbour Station would be much better closer to Shellharbour, wouldn't it?'

The junior station assistant looked at David Hill like he was a bit simple and said, 'No mate, it's much better to have it down here, near the railway line.'

Within weeks of the supremo's visit the station got a name change to Dunmore (Shellharbour).

# A RAILWAY LIFE

*by Chris Holley (with Jim Haynes)*

My earliest railway memories are of holidays with Mum and Dad and my brothers and sister, travelling through the night on the wonderful old mail trains that ran on the western and northern lines of New South Wales. The journeys were from our home at Bathurst in the west, where Dad had joined the New South Wales Railways, to visit our grandmother and aunties at Tamworth in the north.

I remember the dilemma of trying to sleep in a second-class carriage, yet not wanting to miss a minute of our great adventure. I remember the warm, settling glow of the steam engine's smoke-box reflected on the side of the hundreds of cuttings between our home and 'the big city'.

Over the steel and timber bridges we'd go, hearing and counting the clickety-clacks of the rails and the many and varied 'clunks' and 'thuds' as we sped across countless crossover points at unknown stations and sidings. The warm comfort of being wrapped in one of Mum's Onkaparinga blankets failed to bring on slumber – we didn't want to miss a thing.

Returning to Bathurst from Tamworth, I recall the excitement of crossing the old Hawkesbury River Bridge, when the train would slow to a 'walk', and feeling the great steel structure gently swaying as our train made its way tentatively across the void.

What joy it was to be a kid in the 1940s, arriving at mighty Central Station and watching the fabulous little gas-driven platform trucks pulling long strings of open wagons to collect the brake-van luggage and goods. They snaked their way through hundreds of disembarking passengers and never collected one.

After Dad's appointment to Thirroul, on the South Coast, there are the memories of little tank engines hauling innumerable suburban-type rail carriages at what seemed incredible speeds, either engine leading or tender-first. I couldn't help marvelling at the reliability and tenacity of those mighty little workhorses.

Our home in Thirroul was less than a stone's throw from the railway shunting yards. The timber and fibro house shook violently every night when the enormous D57 and D58 steam freight engines chose to 'knock the fires down' directly opposite. Yet, as with any constant sound I suppose, us kids slept soundly through it all, night after night. After all, we were railway kids.

I will never forget the early morning school trains to Wollongong, catching the silvery rays of the rising sun over a still ocean as they steamed through the magnificent scenery around Stanwell Park, with

'Over the steel and timber bridges we'd go.' DF

X510

# CERTIFICATE OF SERVICE

DEPARTMENT OF RAILWAYS

NEW SOUTH WALES

TRAFFIC BRANCH

**THIS CERTIFICATE IS GIVEN WITHOUT ALTERATION OR ERASURE OF ANY KIND.**

Name... ... ... | NICHOLS, Raymond George

### PARTICULARS OF SERVICE

| OCCUPATION | FROM | TO |
|---|---|---|
| Temporary Junior Porter | 2. 6.1925 | 8. 6.1925 |
| Junior Porter | 9. 6.1925 | 1.11.1930 |
| Porter | 2.11.1930 | 30. 6.1935 |
| Leading Porter | 1. 7.1935 | 1. 9.1935 |
| Signalman | 2. 9.1935 | 30.12.1935 |
| Porter in Charge | 31.12.1935 | 31.10.1936 |
| Night Officer | 1.11.1936 | 7. 9.1938 |
| Assistant Station Master | 8. 9.1938 | 20. 6.1947 |
| Station Master | 21. 6.1947 | 1.11.1968 |

Cause of leaving ... ... | RETIRED

CONDUCT SATISFACTORY

53582  7.63  K 1065

Sydney 10 March, 1969.

CHIEF TRAFFIC MANAGER
Head of Branch

Signature of Applicant

A railway life – the late Ray Nicholls' railway career was typical of many.

breathtaking views of the Pacific Ocean. I remember, too, the sight of the coal-stage shunter making its numerous ascents of the Thirroul coal stage. And then, of course, there were the stories Dad told us of his work on the railway.

In 1952 there was much excitement when Dad received word of his appointment as driver to Werris Creek. At the time there were devastating floods all over the state, particularly around Singleton and Maitland, so it was decided that the family would travel by aeroplane to their new home.

Flying on the old Avro of East–West Airlines, at the tender age of thirteen, I observed the magnitude of the flooding first-hand when the pilot flew us low over the flooded areas. From the air there appeared to be one complete silvery lake stretching from Maitland to Singleton.

I can still recall standing on the north-west platform at Werris Creek Station with my mum, sister Yvonne and brothers Greg and Lindsay. All four of us kids were proudly waiting for Dad to come in from Narrabri on the night North West mail train. It was his trial trip as a driver.

It seemed we waited an age but, at last, there it was!

We saw the headlight flashing through the trees in the vicinity of 'the Gap' and then a racing, pulsating bundle of iron, a NSW Government Railway 'P' Class locomotive, was making its way past the massive Werris Creek grain silo. How proud we all were as it came to a grinding, screeching, steam-filled stop at exactly the right spot on the platform, with my dad in control. I wanted to shout to all and sundry, 'That's my Dad, the driver!'

When the time came to leave school, I joined the railways, together with my brothers. Greg and Lindsay were eventually to find more rewarding employment in other spheres; the railways became my career. You might say the railways have pretty much been my life.

When Werris Creek became our permanent home it was a thriving, economically sound railway town with a workforce of 700 to 800 railway employees. There were no airs and graces about the place, and the friendly, hospitable nature of the town quickly won our hearts.

The railway employees worked and played hard but were generally the salt of the earth. Everyone was equal and people's willingness to assist one another back then is something you can never forget if you're fortunate enough to have been a part of it.

I'll also never forget the manner in which the enginemen welcomed the New Year. Werris Creek would resound to 'cock-a-doodle-doo' played on the whistles of some dozen or so old 'steamers' as they welcomed in the next twelve months at midnight on New Year's Eve.

Parties and dances all over town would wait for those sounds from the locos before singing 'Auld Lang Syne' together. Those wonderful New Year celebrations held a special significance for the warm-hearted working folk of our railway town. It was a very close-knit and caring community.

The pride of Werris Creek Station back then was the magnificent Railway Refreshment Rooms. 'The Great Triple R' had immaculately uniformed staff and highly polished floors in which you could see your own reflection. The stained-glass panelling surrounding the bar area was a thing of beauty and the homemade meat pies sent youngsters like me into raptures.

Travellers were served with a smile and almost military efficiency at tables beautifully set with lace tablecloths and spotless napkins. It was a world of its own, a wonderful symbol of a time that knew good manners and delicious country-style food prepared on the premises – a far cry from the mass-produced junk food of the modern era.

Above 'the ref rooms', as the locals called them, was hotel-type accommodation for weary travellers, impeccably maintained to an exceptional standard by a resident manager, his wife and staff. This building still stands today as a reminder of just how grand travel could be back in the days of steam. It has been reduced to mere offices but perhaps one day it can be restored to some degree of its past glory.

The days of steam were nearing their end when I started to work on the railways and the beginning of diesel domination was at hand, but there were many great stories left to be lived and told.

Chris Holley, the author, as a boy (middle right) with his family. CH

After completing the Intermediate Certificate, I left school and applied to join the New South Wales Government Railways. Like hundreds of other hopefuls I was sent to Sydney to sit for the entrance examination at the Personnel Centre in Pitt Street.

At that time there were thousands of new immigrants to this country also endeavouring to obtain employment. It was fascinating for me to observe and be a part of the integration of these 'new Australians' into the Australian lifestyle and way of doing things.

The written examination for entry to a railway career was really a little farcical. The arithmetic and English papers that needed to be taken required a level of knowledge somewhere between kindergarten and second-class standard of the education system as it was then. Knowing how to manage simple addition and spell basic words seemed to be an indication of superior intelligence in a railway examination.

The system, however, completely discriminated against the poor immigrants. Unable to speak a word of our language, they just sat there totally bewildered.

If they learned nothing else from the exam, the immigrant candidates present when I sat the papers at least learned something about the average Aussie's belief in a 'fair go'. Seeing that I had finished my set papers and noting that I had everything correct, the supervising officer asked me if I would mind 'lending' my answers to a table of Italian lads sitting nearby. This I did, and the 'new Australian' boys copied diligently for over an hour and joined the railways along with me and many other Aussies, all with 100 per cent passes. The supervisor was obviously aware that the lingo would come later on.

I was then sent back to 'the Creek', my hometown, and began my railway career with the lofty title of 'junior porter'. I earned my wages by sweeping platforms, cleaning fires in the waiting rooms, emptying waste bins in the offices, loading and unloading the brake-vans of goods and passenger trains, and assisting passengers from one platform to the other. In this manner I helped to keep the Tamworth Passenger, the Northern Tablelands Express, the Brisbane Express, the North West Mail and the Glen Innes Mail all running efficiently. In short, I performed any chore that was deemed to be beneath the dignity of those in higher grades.

In the winter it was necessary to replace 'foot warmers' at Werris Creek, for the comfort of the hardy travellers being conveyed through the darkness and cold of the northern ranges by train.

Passengers may have been near frozen when the train pulled into Werris Creek, but their 'tootsies' were certainly kept warm for hundreds of miles after departure. The acid-filled rectangular metal containers, which we heated by immersion in boiling water for many hours prior to the arrival of night-time passenger trains, were thrown into each carriage while the train was stopped at Werris Creek.

From this lowly beginning I rose to the position of station assistant, which was a glamorous new name for the old 'porter'. From there it was ever upwards to the dizzy heights of leading station assistant.

In this position I was responsible for the admittance and dispatch of trains through the station. I also assisted with the attaching and detaching of relief engines to the passenger trains, and carrying out safe working duties for all trains at the Werris Creek Railway Station. It was while carrying out the duties laid down in the regulations for this position that I became acutely aware of the idiosyncrasies of railway administration.

One of the less desirable tasks allocated to the leading station assistant was performed when commencing duty on a Sunday afternoon. This was the cleaning of the tar-covered 'urinal' in the men's toilets, and then painting it over with Wollol disinfectant.

One Sunday, after obtaining a bucket from the 'out-of-goods storage room' and filling it with the jet-black Wollol, I walked along the northern platform, not noticing that the bucket had been punctured and had a small hole in the bottom. Having completed the chore, I walked back to the storage room, this time along the north-western platform, and placed the bucket in its designated place.

Several hours later, on the same shift, I walked up to the points levers at the end of the platform to perform another of my duties. This was to turn the 'outgoing' engine for the Armidale to Sydney passenger service from the loop line where it was standing onto the main line, in order to attach it to the passenger train.

In the middle of the operation, I accidentally pulled the line across from under the engine while it was proceeding from one line to the other, totally derailing the unit and almost causing it to fall on its side. It took the breakdown crew many hours to rectify the situation and an extended delay was caused to the passenger train service.

Several days later I received correspondence from the Department calling for my statement about the matter. I admitted my full responsibility and, two weeks after this, was informed that, although I had caused many thousands of dollars worth of damage to the diesel locomotive, there was to be no official reprimand. I should merely be more alert and careful in future.

At the same time I received notification that I was to be severely reprimanded for 'defacing the platform' by spilling a line of disinfectant along its length. I never could, and still cannot to this day, comprehend the wisdom behind those two momentous decisions.

Up the ladder I went again, to the position of shunter. This involved working with a gang of four others under the supervision of a 'yardmaster'. As the lowest of the low in the gang, it was my responsibility to take long rakes of loaded or empty wagons to the bottom of each road in the shunting yard. I was required to tie on sufficient handbrakes to stabilise the train being marshalled.

I also had to take off with due haste after any runaway vehicles and endeavour to stop their progress with a heavy wooden sprag, tapered at either end to allow for it being thrust into the spokes on the rail wagons. Unfortunately, it seemed that every time I was placed in a situation requiring such moves, I was already 50 yards to the rear before I realised it was necessary. I usually watched them disappear into the distance and derail in a rather large cloud of dust, metal and ash.

At the end of an eight-hour turn of duty, especially night work, bed was welcome relief. There were incredible numbers of trains to be shunted back then, and we were, on most occasions, given only a ten-minute meal break on a shift. These breaks were taken individually in order to permit continuity of the related duties. The others in the gang soldiered on with one 'down' at each break.

Shunting was exhausting work, requiring physical fitness and total concentration. Many facets of the job were potentially dangerous and we relied on the care and diligence of our fellow workers to ensure a safe shift every time. The job would have been impossible without the humour, skill and easygoing nature of most of the men who worked in those gangs.

From there I was promoted to the position of guard, a job in which I was to spend over ten years of my life. I thoroughly enjoyed the freedom of that position. I was able to travel all over the north and north-west of New South Wales, through some of the most beautiful countryside in the world, and all in the company of some wonderful workmates. As a guard I witnessed floods, fires, tragedies, derailments and many other memorable incidents. Something seemed to happen on almost every shift.

Working conditions were spartan back then. Running staff employees (drivers, firemen and guards) were required to work virtually unlimited hours per fortnight, with a maximum of eleven hours off duty and eight hours when sleeping over in a 'foreign' depot barracks. These rules applied even though men would often have been on duty for over fifteen hours, travelling to the opposite end of the line or working trains home.

In the city there were call-cars to meet the trains and take men home after a shift. In the bush, however, when a man was relieved at his working shift limit of eleven or twelve hours, he was required to travel the rest of the way in the train brake-van.

Rail traffic through the Werris Creek depot in the '50s and '60s was at saturation point. Today's trains haul an average of 4130 tons but back then steam trains hauled an average load of 675 tons – so trains were running day and night and, in many instances, every half-hour. Down to Broadmeadow went dozens of trains every day, with wheat, timber, coal, barley, ore, stock and general goods.

Men were called for duty as soon as their allotted 'sleep allowance' had expired, and this could be at any hour of the day or night. A complete night at home in bed was a 'luxury' to be treasured.

A man's body takes great exception to the constraints placed upon it by continually eating and sleeping at irregular hours. I recall being awoken from a sleep of total exhaustion at 2 am one morning to sign on duty 'as soon as possible'. I am not ashamed to admit that I sat on the end of my bed crying, my body literally shaking from lack of catch-up sleep.

One fortnight I worked 146 actual hours around the clock and in a semi-stupor. In the same pay-period a young guard, who was two years my senior at the time, worked 151 actual hours. Three days later, while taking particulars of the load of his train in Werris Creek shunting yard, he collapsed and died of a heart attack. Lack of sleep and stress were obviously contributing factors in his untimely death.

Railway barracks were mostly dilapidated structures, with little or no coverings on wooden floors whose boards were coming apart after years of neglect. In winter the winds crept through the gaps to freeze many a traumatised body trying to catch forty winks. Barracks were also renowned for wet sheets and paper-thin blankets that wouldn't cover a garden gnome. Of course, they were always beside the track, shunting yards and fuel depots, and were mostly noisy.

When the new diesels began their forays into the north, there were many extensive delays to steam trains, which caused major timetable disruptions and meant many nights in barracks for running staff. Diesels were regarded as 'blue ribbon' trains and had priority running. All delays were meticulously recorded and action was taken against any employee found guilty of delaying them.

Departing Muswellbrook one evening with a steam-hauled general goods train, we arrived at Scone Railway Station where the assistant stationmaster informed me that he was stowing my train in the station stockyards siding. The siding was just outside the actual station yard and he told me my train would be there for about three hours, to allow several of the new diesel trains to 'run through and maintain their timetables'.

We waited so long, as it turned out, that the whole crew fell asleep and the fire went out in the loco. The train controller had rubbed us off his board and forgotten to put us back on, and the assistant stationmaster had forgotten us and left us there from 10 am until 6 am the next morning.

Of course, goods trains also had to make way for passenger trains. One Sunday evening, travelling from Werris Creek to Narrabri, our train arrived at the unattended Curlewis Station. A call from the train controller directed us to turn my train into the 'silo road', to allow the Moree-to-Sydney passenger train to pass.

The silo road was used to stow long goods trains. Admittance to the siding was gained by holding down a set of 'ball points'. These points were so named because there was a heavy steel ball on the bottom of the lever. It required a feat of some considerable strength to hold the handle down and allow the points leading to the desired siding to adopt the required position.

As I weighed over 14 stone I simply sat on the handle and signalled the driver to proceed into the siding. It was a still, dark night with no moon, but the engine and leading wagons passed me smoothly and everything appeared to be normal.

Suddenly the night air was filled with the sound of a thousand banshees wailing! There was a screeching, the scream of rending metal, an enormous thump ... then all was silent.

The train was derailed, trucks were telescoped into others, and several were lying at rakish angles, horizontal to the track. It was a picture of utter destruction.

I was certain I never moved on the points; there must've been some other cause. Perhaps the rails had spread. I immediately ran over to the railway station and reported the derailment to the control officer on the phone. I then called out the stationmaster, who, of course, was off duty for the day.

Within an hour the fettling gangs, breakdown crews and inspectors from the perway (that is, permanent way), locomotive and traffic sections of local administrative offices had all arrived and endeavoured to determine the cause of the pile-up.

'Diesels were regarded as "blue ribbon" trains and had priority running.' DF

An inquiry was held and the blame was placed fairly and squarely on my shoulders. The Railway Board ruled that I 'had moved whilst seated on the points'. I was devastated. I was absolutely certain that I had not moved an inch on those darn points that night.

Enter the Good Samaritan, in the shape of the Curlewis stationmaster whose rest had been so rudely interrupted that night. Signing on duty for another job while still awaiting my punishment for the derailment, I was advised to ring Curlewis urgently as the stationmaster had 'certain information' regarding the incident.

He informed me that he had overheard a conversation in the dark at the scene of the derailment that night, between the perway inspector and the locomotive engineer. The gist of the conversation was that the derailment had obviously been caused by 'blunt leads on the points', coupled with a 'sharp flange' on the leading wheel of a petroleum wagon close behind the engine. This combination of factors had caused the loaded fuel truck to 'mount the rails' and topple over.

'It required a feat of some considerable strength to hold the handle down.' DF

If the truth came out the 'blame' would have been shared between two branches of the Department. The mechanical branch would be blamed for not checking and detecting the sharp flange on the vehicle; the perway branch would be blamed for failing to observe the blunt lead on the points. The two officers in question had made a pact to lay the blame on the guard and fix their problems the following day.

The stationmaster had been stewing on this information for several days and, with his conscience troubling him, he made a decision to let me know the facts and to support me when I reported the matter. Men of such character and applaudable honesty were not uncommon back then.

I duly notified the senior officer in the depot and there was no further action taken in my direction from the administration. I trust, however, that a swift kick in the pants was aimed in two other directions.

I have many other memories of my time on the railways; after all,

*Left:* A typical 1960s station crew – Stationmaster Russel Bright (left) and staff at Coonabarabran. RB/EP

*Below:* Shunting was exhausting work. DF

'Who would have believed that the little boy who used to dream of train journeys … would one day have such an enormous train set to control.' DF

I spent my entire working life on New South Wales railways. There were lots of laughs and good times, but the hard times leave strong memories.

I vividly recall spending an hour and a half in Walcha Road station yards one bitterly cold night shovelling deep snow from all the points in the yard leading to the various wagon sites, to enable shunting to continue. We were there for over five hours due to the terrible conditions.

I dreaded working the 'pick-up' train from Werris Creek to Armidale and returning on the 'up' pick-up. That job was sheer murder: on the forward journey, the guard often 'walked' most of the hundred miles up the mountains. Shunting was required at almost every station along the track.

To make things even more interesting, as a guard I was required to unload wool packs and various heavy consigned items at tiny isolated platforms – in most instances with only the cherished assistance of the train's fireman. After working those type of twelve-hour shifts an atom bomb wouldn't have disturbed you when your head finally hit the pillow at Armidale barracks, or on arrival back home if you were lucky.

There were similar pick-up trains operating in every direction from Werris Creek, all at night. It was hard yakka, and all successfully accomplished by a team of just three men working each train. Any customer was welcome to send any item of goods by rail then, from a loaf of bread to enormous electrical transformers. Nothing was knocked back. We took pride in delivering everything safely and, in the majority of cases, promptly.

After many years working as a guard, I eventually found my way into the control section of the railways at Werris Creek. That was a traumatic lifestyle change. I had to make on-the-spot decisions and tax my old brain to the limit as there were trains running all over the north and north-west. The whole northern district was a hive of activity through the '50s, '60s and '70s. It was a period of unbelievable growth for the railways.

Through good times, droughts, floods and tempest, the trains kept coming and going, and there I was, controlling them as best I could. Who would have believed that the little boy who used to dream of train journeys wrapped in his mum's old Onkaparinga blanket all those years ago would one day have such an enormous train set to control and direct? You should never stop your kids from dreaming and imagining, because sometimes dreams come true.

# 1174

*Anon*

When you're signing on at Enfield and they meet you at the door
And they tell you that your engine is 1174,
You can hear the driver grumble; you can hear the fireman roar …
Why? Just look in the repair book of 1174.

'Faulty valves and pistons', 'burnt-off smoke box door',
'Engine steaming badly' … that's 1174.
God knows why they run her, but the bosses know what's best,
She'll be hours late any time they run her to the west.

And if they put her on a north job you can always safely bet
That she'll end up in a siding somewhere up near Morisset.
Try to take her 'cross the mountains where she really has to climb!
By the time you get to Glenbrook you're an hour behind time!

I have struggled, sworn and sweated, I have tried to get her through,
But I always feel like quitting when I get to Warrimoo!
'Cos we're facing those Blue Mountains and we'll do the best we can,
But to make that engine steam well is a task beyond a man!

'Engine steaming badly – that's 1174.' 1174 was renumbered as a 54 class loco, as shown here. DF

*I take up that damn shovel, off come my overalls,*
*And I know that I'll be buggered when we get to Wentworth Falls.*
*As we struggle on to Lithgow we swear and curse our fate,*
*And 1174 is just exactly three hours late.*

*It's a number that will haunt me and haunt me evermore,*
*For it doesn't matter what I do … it's 1174.*
*One night my dear wife said to me, 'Your hands are burnt and sore!'*
*I said, 'Yes, I've been to Lithgow on 1174.'*

*She gave me perfumed soap for them, the best she could procure,*
*It's called '4711' … just like 1174!*
*I bought a ticket in the lottery, thought my luck would change for sure,*
*The winner was 1175 … I had 1174!*

*Disgusted I enlisted and went off to the war*
*And my regimental number was 1174.*
*And when the war was ended I came back to work once more*
*And they sent me off to Lithgow on 1174!*

# ALWAYS LATE

*by Russell Hannah & Jim Haynes*

'Bloody trains, always late,' said Henry the Hun.

Henry had just joined the table and was in the process of drinking his first beer of the evening. Evidently, he'd been in the city for the day and had caught the train home. Of course, it had been twenty minutes late – this was never exactly an unexpected event. The train home was late more often than it was on time. Henry, however, always seemed somewhat affronted that this should be the case.

Henry was a creature of habit. His displeasure was mostly caused by the fact that he couldn't stand being late for his nightly drinking session. For one thing, he worried that Leo the Lover might talk about him in his absence.

In fact, Leo the Lover rarely talked about Henry when he wasn't there, but he never missed a chance to stir him when he was present. And he wasn't about to let this opportunity pass.

'Hitler and Mussolini got the trains to run on time,' Leo remarked slyly. He liked to have a little jibe at Henry's Teutonic background whenever he could.

The reference to fascism may have been a bit too subtle for Henry, who was still preoccupied savouring his first beer of the night. He ignored it.

'There wasn't a great deal happening in the town, so most of the population was at the station.' WCL

'You don't know what a late train is,' Leo persisted. 'Have you ever heard about the infamous South West Mail, the latest train in New South Wales railway history?'

Leo has a story about almost anything and everything to do with railways. 'The South West Mail,' he began, as he lowered his glass, straightened his shoulders and took up his storytelling position, 'was never on time. In fact, it was due in at one small country town at 8.50 am and the people there used to sort of check their clocks by it. If their watches showed 8.50 am and the train was in, then they knew that their watches needed adjusting.

'You see the old mail had never trundled into that particular station on time for well over five years. It was a standing joke in the town. The publican of the town's only pub – which was of course called the Railway Hotel – used to run a daily sweepstake. Punters had to guess what time the train would arrive. Only the most optimistic would have it in before 10.50 am, which was only two hours late.'

Leo took a rather large swig from his schooner. 'One day the unthinkable happened.' He paused for effect. 'The train chugged in *on time*. There was astonishment at the Railway Hotel. Naturally, it was a skinner for the publican. No one had picked the correct time.

'The publican was a bloke by the name of O'Flaherty. Having some Irish in him, he enjoyed a bit of a celebration and a party. He also liked to talk and was fond of making speeches.

'The opportunity was too good to resist. He quickly sent the message around town that there would be a celebration and an award made down at the station to the driver.

'There wasn't a great deal happening in the town so most of the population were at the station well before O'Flaherty arrived with a box of beer and a bottle of scotch. He had, after all, had a great result in the sweep and he was a good-hearted fellow, for a publican.

'The driver was busy cleaning out the ash box and was a bit startled to see such a gathering confronting him.

'I don't know exactly what O'Flaherty said,' Leo went on, 'but it was along the lines of: it was a great day for the town … an historic first … it had put the town on the map … the driver was a man of great skill and integrity … and a good bloke to boot … and he had the full appreciation of everyone in the town.

'He then presented the driver with the beer and the scotch, as a token of his appreciation and the great esteem that he was now held in by the townspeople. The crowd applauded and O'Flaherty proposed three cheers for the driver, which everyone enthusiastically delivered.

'Well, at first the driver was puzzled by all this attention. He looked a little sheepish, and then he became suspicious. It had occurred to him that O'Flaherty, who he knew well, was having a bit of a shot at him, attempting to make fun of him in front of the whole town. As the ceremony proceeded, however, he realised the awful truth – these people really did think the train was on time.

'The driver was an honest sort of bloke and his face began to go red with embarrassment. When the cheers subsided and everyone looked at him expectantly, he realised they were waiting for him to reply. The poor bloke had never felt so embarrassed in his life, but he decided honesty was the best policy.

'"I'm sorry, friends," he said. "I'd love to accept this scotch and beer for such a mighty achievement but my dear old mother was a staunch Presbyterian and she taught me not to lie. I cannot accept this reward."

'A gasp ran through the crowd. In the deep silence that followed, the driver continued: "The reason I can't accept this award is that this train is not on time, even though it pulled into the station at the scheduled arrival time of 8.50 am. I know it means missing out on the reward, but I have to confess that this is not this morning's train. It's yesterday's train …"'

'What happened then?' I asked.

'Well,' said Leo, 'the crowd was stunned, although there were some among them who said that they knew it had to be wrong in the first place. Only a miracle would have caused the train to be on time, and people living in small country towns don't really believe in miracles.

'O'Flaherty was impressed by the driver's honesty and invited everyone back to the pub, where they knocked over the case of beer and quite a few more cases as well. But one thing they did do as a result of the incident was to put a chart on the wall with the timetable on it. After that they always ticked off the last train into town, so if the train ever got to be a few days late they couldn't be caught out again.'

'That's not a bad story,' said Henry the Hun, who had been waiting to get his share of the talking action. 'But I've a better one than that. This story is about the old "Ghan". It travelled on a three-foot-six gauge track from Port Augusta, through Maree and Oodnadatta to Alice Springs, and took anything from two days to two months to get there.

'The Ghan even had its own theme song. During the war the troops all sang "I'll Walk Beside You". They reckoned it wasn't a timetable that the driver had to stick to; it was a calendar. Drivers on the Ghan always carried a rifle as well – they had to shoot game to feed the passengers if the train got stranded in the floods.

'One time in the mid '70s the country flooded and the Ghan went missing for six weeks. The Alice Springs newspaper held a competition: contestants had to nominate what year, month, day and hour the Ghan would arrive. When it finally did arrive, the biggest crowd ever to meet the Ghan was waiting on Alice Springs Station. The crowd were all looking at their watches but the passengers thought the Alice must be the friendliest town in the world! Which of course it used to be.

'And that's a true story, too,' added Henry, with a sideways glance at Leo. 'A friend of my Great Uncle Herman was the stationmaster at the time it happened. Lots of funny things happened on that train.

'One time, when the Ghan pulled into the Alice, the conductor jumped off the train in an agitated state. "Quick! Get a doctor," he said to my great uncle's mate. "There's a woman onboard and she's about to have a baby!"

'Well, the stationmaster immediately rang through to the hospital and a doctor was there within minutes. He delivered the baby girl and all was well.

'Bloody trains, always late …' Late trains are always a political issue. NSW PTU

Souvenir postcard of the old Ghan passing through 'the Gap'.

'The old Ghan travelled on a three-foot-six gauge track from Port Augusta to Alice Springs and took anything from two days to two months to get there.' NTL NTGP

'The doc, however, was none too pleased with the woman and gave her a bit of a serve. "Madam," he said after the delivery, "that was irresponsible; you should never have got on the train in your condition."

'The woman looked at the doctor sadly and said, "Doctor, when I got on the train I wasn't in this condition!"

'Now, that's a late train!' Henry concluded.

'Well, I hope we're not too late for another beer,' said Leo, 'because it's your shout.'

# THE RUNAWAY TRAIN

*by Grahame Watt*

*The train roared down the mountain, the engine driver paled,*
*He bellowed at the fireman, 'The flaming brakes have failed!'*
*The train raced on freewheeling, the whistle warned ahead,*
*Around the bends at break-neck speed, through signals green and red.*

*Faster, ever faster, the driver tried in vain!*
*He pulled every lever but he couldn't stop that train.*
*It hurtled across bridges and crossings in a flash,*
*At a hundred miles an hour upon its downward dash.*

*Sparks came off the spinning wheels; the guard began to swear,*
*The driver and the fireman said a silent prayer.*
*Then slowly, very slowly, for the mountains had now gone,*
*The speed began to slacken, but still the train rolled on.*

*The further that it travelled from that mad descent,*
*The further that the train rolled free, the slower that it went*
*For forty miles the train slowed down, on level ground once more,*
*Till it stopped at Central Station, platform twenty-four.*

'The train roared down the mountain ...' DF

*Well the driver was a hero; they still talk of the day,*
*The Minister for Railways had quite a lot to say.*
*'This is a special day,' he said, 'a day of joy sublime,*
*For it is the first occasion that this train has run ON TIME!'*

# THE MAN WHO CONQUERED THE MOUNTAINS

*by Jim Haynes*

Ask an Aussie to name the Yorkshireman best known in Australia and you would probably be told (at least by those who knew where Yorkshire was) either Captain James Cook or Freddy Truman. Ask a hundred New South Welshmen who John Whitton was and I doubt one would know the answer.

Thousands of commuters each day pass by the bronze bust of John Whitton at Central Station in Sydney without a second glance. It's a shame, really, that we have almost forgotten 'the father of the New South Wales Railways'.

John Whitton was born near Wakefield, Yorkshire, in 1819. His father was a land agent and the family lived in a village with the rather unpromising, although perhaps typically Yorkshire, name of Foulby. Yorkshire was at the centre of the Industrial Revolution and young John's uncle ran a successful engineering business. It was there he was apprenticed and became skilled at preparing construction plans for railways and waterworks.

Extremely capable and practical in his manner, and with an impressive work ethic, Whitton began to specialise in railways and, at just twenty-eight, was engineer on the Manchester, Sheffield and

Lincoln Railway. By 1852, at the age of thirty-three, his reputation was such that he was chosen to replace the greatest engineer of them all, Isambard Brunel, as resident engineer on the Oxford, Worcester and Wolverhampton Railway.

Until the age of thirty-six, John Whitton seems to have had few interests except his work. He was almost the archetypal dour Yorkshireman, working at a job at which he was skilled and well-suited, in close proximity to his birthplace. This was all about to change.

On the other side of the world, in the far-distant British colony of New South Wales, until recently a convict settlement, events were astir that would lead John Whitton into a new life of unimagined adventures and achievements. It happened that Lord Stanley, the president of the Board of Trade, had been asked for assistance by the colony. They were looking for a promising man to go out to that still unexplored land and build the colony's railway system.

There were already railways in New South Wales. The Sydney to Parramatta line had been built by the Sydney Railway Company and opened in 1855, and there was a line being constructed by the Hunter River Railway Company in the Hunter Valley, from East to West Maitland. There had been many problems with these railways, however, and, in December 1854, Charles FitzRoy's last act as governor-general of the colonies had been to give assent to a bill that acquired these railways for the government and made provision for the government to construct and own all future railways in the colony.

New South Wales had been granted responsible government in 1855 and the new government needed an engineer-in-chief, someone with a practical knowledge of railway planning, costing and construction; someone who could deal with inexperienced colonial politicians. They needed 'a thoroughly practical engineer of considerable professional attainments' and 'a gentleman of unquestioned principle and integrity'. That was exactly how the powerful British railway magnate Sir Morgan Peto described John Whitton in his recommendation to Lord Stanley.

The following year, 1856, was a momentous one for John Whitton. For a start, at the age of thirty-six, he married Elizabeth Fowler, the sister of his old boss on the Manchester, Sheffield and Lincoln Railway. Then he was offered, and accepted, the commission to become engineer-in-chief of the New South Wales Government Railways at an annual salary of £1500. Later that year he sailed for Australia with his new bride.

Sir William Denison was the new governor of New South Wales. He was a professional soldier with a background in engineering. John Whitton would need to display considerable amounts of his Yorkshire stubbornness in the months and years to come.

There were two early battles that Whitton needed to win. Firstly, Denison had suggested a horse-drawn rail system for the more remote areas of the colony. Not long after his arrival, in fact the day after his appointment was officially confirmed by the Railway Board, Whitton stated:

> I would not recommend any line to be made to be worked by horsepower. Any gradient which is bad for locomotives will be bad for horses also. You must take into consideration the immense amount of horse labour you have to employ to execute the same amount of work you would get done by a locomotive engine. I think it would not be by any means a saving but a great additional expense.

Whitton also showed he was a man who was willing to speak his mind, whether Governor Denison liked it or not, on the issue of surveys. Until that time, railway surveys had been conducted by military personnel under the charge of the surveyor-general, in the same way that land surveys were conducted. In spite of the governor's military-engineering background, Whitton was blunt in his opinion of the surveys conducted thus far: 'I think they are being carried out in a very objectionable manner so far as the railway is concerned. I think decidedly that they should be under the charge of the Engineer of Railways. I do not see what the Surveyor-General can have to do with them.'

The bronze bust of John Whitton
at Central Station, Sydney. RH

The man himself. NSW SA

You can almost hear the Yorkshire accent in such direct quotes. As John Gunn puts it in his excellent railway history *Along Parallel Lines*, 'forceful argument, bluntly expressed, was the Whitton way.'

John Whitton also had the foresight to predict the calamity that would one day ensue from the various colonies not getting together on gauges and railway construction. He told the NSW premier, Charles Cowper: 'If you ever do join you will find it a great inconvenience … from here to South Australia you would be forced to have two changes of carriage. But this would be trifling compared with the expense and trouble attending the changing of goods from one gauge to another.'

He himself favoured the gauge used in Victoria: 5 foot 3 inches. When forced to compromise to a narrower gauge, with politicians recommending gauges as narrow as 2 feet, he drew the line in the sand at 'standard gauge' – 4 foot 8½ inches – and wrote to Railways Commissioner John Rae: 'I must express my decided opinion that any reduction would be attended with the most serious inconvenience and cause great loss of revenue … a very large traffic on all the lines will be derived from the carriage of livestock and I assert that no traffic of this description can be carried economically on a less gauge than 4 feet 8½ inches.'

He succeeded, in the face of political opposition, in keeping all New South Wales railways to the same gauge. *The Town and Country Journal* wrote a tribute to Whitton in September 1878, a decade before he retired, and reminded its readers that 'he maintained this view in opposition to a select committee … and events have proved that he was right.'

Whitton also brought common sense to bear in the matter of tendering for railway construction 'in the English market, where they would get the large contractors to compete'. This also meant that much expertise, plant and labour were brought into the colony at the expense of the successful contractors. This did, indeed, prove to be a successful practice. There was certainly no labour force available in New South Wales at the time and, naturally, many of these railway-building immigrants made the colony their permanent home, as did Whitton himself.

When politicians asked him why these labourers couldn't be paid at the same rates as they were in Britain – that is, significantly less than Whitton intended to pay them in Australia – that Yorkshire common sense again shone through: 'If the contractor were to bring out ten thousand men he could not keep them at so low a rate of wages. If you take men from a country where the average rate of wages is three shillings a day and bring them to one where the average is nine shillings, you cannot expect those men to stay with you at the lower rate.'

When it came to planning railway routes, John Whitton was renowned for being incorruptible and beyond the bribery of ambitious politicians and greedy landowners. His brother-in-law, by now Sir John Fowler, acted as inspector of the railway materials before they were dispatched from England, as a result of which Whitton was at one time accused of nepotism. Not only was he subsequently cleared of any impropriety but it would soon become apparent that Whitton had indeed chosen the right man for the job, for, after Sir John retired and tenders were accepted from another company, the new materials were found to be very inferior and not made to the specifications laid down.

Rural industry pioneer Thomas Mort was certainly impressed with Whitton. He even 'congratulated the colony' for having an engineer at the head of its Railway Department 'who has not permitted his judgment to be interfered with by any external pressure, or popular attempt to mislead'.

If Whitton's style was, as John Gunn says, 'uncompromising and often harsh', it was also true that he was 'as dour and as abrupt with his superiors as he was with those under him'. Commissioner Rae said of him: 'He never courted popularity, and the stern justice of his decisions may have given offence to some persons; but he was a great favourite with all who acted with, or under him, in the railway department, and was most admired by those who knew him best.'

Whitton made alterations to locomotive design which enabled them to burn coal instead of wood. This was a great advance as the cinders from wood often caused damage to passengers' clothes and property along the lines. He also instituted modern systems of account-keeping for the various branches he set up for railway administration – the locomotive and carriage branches, track maintenance and workshops.

Even without all these remarkable achievements, John Whitton would have gone down in history as one of the world's greatest engineers on the basis of one phenomenal accomplishment: taking the railway across the Great Dividing Range on what would become known as 'the Great Zig Zag'. The Blue Mountains, that section of the Great Dividing Range just west of Sydney, had provided a barrier to the colony's development since the first settlement in 1788. It was twenty-five years before the mountains were even officially crossed, after which that enlightened governor, Lachlan Macquarie, wasted no time in having a road built, in 1815, and establishing Bathurst as the first inland town that same year. By 1860, however, this route – Cox's famous convict-built road – was the only link between the Port of Sydney and the prosperous inland farming areas and the coal and iron ore deposits found in the Lithgow Valley. The colony's development was slowed to the pace of bullock teams. John Whitton changed all that when he took the railway across the Great Dividing Range.

Penrith, 35 miles from Sydney, is just 88 feet above sea level. From there the railway had to climb 3658 feet in just over 50 miles to enter the proposed Clarence Tunnel. The construction of this line, including the first zigzag at Lapstone Hill, and its continuation west via the Great Zig Zag into the Lithgow Valley, was one of the greatest engineering and construction feats of the Victorian age.

The idea itself was simple – build a track in the form of a giant Z. The train would come along the top or bottom of the Z to a set of points, switch back down the middle to another set of points and then forward again on its way. It would take a lot of shunting and engines would have to 'run around' their trains, making it a slow process, but it would make previously impossible grades possible. The trick was to find a way to carve the two giant Zs into the incredibly wild, rugged terrain of the Blue Mountains.

Whitton began by designing the first zigzag, which raised the line 520 feet to the summit of Lapstone Hill. To do this, he had to design and build a three-span bridge over the Nepean River and a massive stone viaduct across Knapsack Gully. The bridge, named the Victoria Bridge (naturally), had three spans of 200 feet, and the viaduct required seven arches and rose 126 feet at its centre. The steepest gradient here was one in thirty. The construction of this zigzag was mere child's play, however, when compared to the building of the one that was necessary on the western side of the Great Dividing Range.

The Lithgow Valley zigzag – the Great Zig-Zag – carried the line from the Clarence Tunnel down a descent of 687 feet to the valley floor in three great sweeps across the mountainsides. The gradient was one in forty-two and Commissioner John Rae wrote that it 'passed through a deep and rugged ravine where formerly there was scarcely footing for the mountain goat and where the surveyors' assistants had occasionally to be suspended by ropes in the performance of their perilous duties'. John Whitton himself spent many hours sitting in a basket hung over these enormous spectacular cliffs while he surveyed and checked the progress of the construction.

An old colleague of Whitton's, George Cowdery, was the resident engineer for this section of the line. Cowdery had worked under Whitton building the Oxford, Worcester and Wolverhampton Railway in Britain. He emigrated to Victoria in 1856, during the gold rushes, and had worked as an engineer on the Melbourne to Bendigo line. Many British workers, including over 2000 Scots, both skilled and unskilled, arrived in the colony to help build the line across the mountains.

Construction lasted three years, from 1866 to 1869, and the project was a source of fascination in the colony. In January 1867, part of the mountain blocking the line near the first reversing station of the Great Zig Zag needed to be removed by blasting. This was to be the most massive explosion ever seen in Australia. Using the new process of electrical detonation, 40 000 tons of rock were to be cleared in one huge blast. Twenty-five holes were drilled 30 feet into the mountain face and over 3 tons of blasting powder were inserted.

It became a great social occasion and the theatrical nature of the event, on 5 January, was enhanced by two failed attempts at detonation. The first attempt was at one o'clock, and the second some thirty minutes later. Finally, at five minutes to two, after more wire had been replaced, the third attempt was successful. The governor's wife, Lady Belmore, pushed the detonator and the resulting explosion, in Commissioner Rae's words, 'tore the mountain asunder, heaving huge masses of rock into the valley ... leaving the face of the parent mountain almost as plain as if it had been cut with chisels'.

After the entertaining event, celebration followed, as *The Sydney Morning Herald* reported: 'a large number of ladies from different parts of the district being in the immediate vicinity by invitation ... the party, numbering upwards of fifty persons, sat down to an excellent luncheon served in No. 1 Tunnel. A better or cooler place for a luncheon, considering the intense heat of the weather, could not be conceived.'

The line was completed with much fanfare in September 1869. A reporter from *The Empire* newspaper described his first trip on the Great Zig Zag:

> *[The] descent is commenced along the back of the tortuous ridge dividing the impassable gullies descending on the right to the Grose River and on the left to Cox's River … approaching the verge of the precipices where the Zig-Zag commences … the various traverses of the line are seen crossing each other at intervals below and to look down from the windows of the railway carriages almost makes the traveller dizzy. The track runs along the side of the cliffs cut through the solid rock in most places, in others carried on lofty arches of masonry …*

Many thousands of passengers had similar feelings of awe and excitement while making the journey across the mountains by rail. Finally, as Henry Lawson said, 'The flaunting flag of progress is in the West unfurled, The mighty bush with iron rails is tethered to the world.' Now goods and passengers and mail could flow across the mountains in either direction. The port of Sydney and overseas markets were open to primary products; inland isolation was overcome; the city and the bush could come together in new developments. News and letters were only a day or two away for people of the Western Plains. Mail was sorted on the trains as they sped through the night to the west.

While Lawson bemoaned the passing of the 'golden days' of bush life, Banjo Paterson celebrated the new era of a communication to the remotest parts of the bush:

> *By rock and ridge and riverside the Western Mail has gone,*
> *Across the great Blue Mountain Range to take the letter on.*
> *A moment on the topmost grade while open fire doors glare,*

'The track runs along the side of the cliffs ... carried on lofty arches of masonry.' ARHS NSW RRC

*She pauses like a living thing to breathe the mountain air.*
*Then launches down the other side across the plains away*
*To bear that note to 'Conroy's sheep, along the Castlereagh'.*

In the building of this railway the colony truly came of age. No longer a quaint colonial backwater, the colony of New South Wales now had an engineering marvel to impress the world, along with all the strange plants, animals and natural wonders.

Many people were mightily impressed, and not just the locals. French diplomat Edmond La Meslee, for instance, wrote a wonderful account of crossing the mountains by train in 1880:

*Leaving the little town of Penrith, the line crosses the Nepean on a splendid iron bridge. Beyond the Emu Plains siding, the country changes in character: a line of tall mountains rises like a veritable wall, shutting off access to the rich tablelands and plains of the interior. To climb the first escarpment, the railway engineers designed a very ingenious zigzag system which enables relatively high speeds to be maintained. This zigzag section is not as complex as that at Lithgow, where the line descends on the other side of the Mountains. As the altitude increases, the horizon extends to embrace the entire plain below, enclosed in a vast circle of hills ending at the entrance to Sydney Harbour, which can be seen with a good telescope.*

*The line continues climbing along the mountainsides in this way and then keeps to the top of the ridge for about thirty miles. One after the other we passed through charming little villages like Woodburn, Lawson and Mount Victoria, where wealthy Sydney people maintain attractive country houses for their summer holidays. People appreciate the mountain climate keenly: European fruits grow there freely and in winter the temperature falls to freezing point. The pretty little town of Mount Victoria, in a sense the centre of the district, boasts a hotel that would not disgrace a provincial town in France.*

*Beyond Mount Victoria the line continues to follow the crest of the Blue Mountains till it begins to descend the western slopes. Here we came to the second zigzag, the masterpiece of Australian engineering.*

*It seems miraculous that human brains and brawn should have been able to conceive and construct the zigzag along the fearful face of this escarpment. The mountainside falls away dizzyingly here, and when the engineers made their first preliminary surveys, they had to be lowered down the precipice by ropes to measure their angles. Later, to build the three viaducts that carry the line, the workmen in their turn had to work on the foundations, while dangling suspended by ropes from above. The wild and rugged landscape contrasts with that enjoyed by the traveller between Lawson and Mount Victoria, where he looks out over an ocean of variegated greenery.*

*The locomotive slowed down to negotiate this difficult section of the line. We passed through a short tunnel and the train stopped. Before backing down to the beginning of the second leg of the zigzag, the driver sounded a strident blast of the whistle, that re-echoed eerily from the abyss, to warn the men working lower down on the line of the train's impending arrival. The coaches skidded on the rails but were controlled by powerful brakes. One shuddered to think what terrible accidents could occur on such gradients without those safety precautions.*

*The train stopped a second time, negotiated the third zigzag, and soon we were bowling along on the valley floor. Alongside the line flowed a little stream with flowering bushes growing on its banks. To see the crest of the mountainside, more than a thousand feet above, one had to lean right out of the window. In fact, until the train entered the Lithgow valley, it was not easy to catch a glimpse of a patch of blue sky.*

For forty years from 1869 every train across the mountains in either direction used John Whitton's zigzags. By 1910, however, traffic was so heavy that bottlenecks delayed trains constantly and there were some spectacular, though relatively harmless, accidents. A new line was designed, using what became known as 'the ten-tunnel deviation'. The old track was torn up and the bush slowly reclaimed the land. Where the great scar of the railway had existed since the massive destruction of bushland in the 1860s, peaceful walking tracks through new-growth forest were all that remained of the engineering marvel of its age.

But the story wasn't finished. It is still possible to ride the Great Zig Zag today.

In 1972 a group of railway enthusiasts started to rebuild the track and then formed a co-operative and purchased rolling stock. Trains first ran again on part of the line in 1975. The track was extended all the way to Clarence in 1988 with the aid of a Bicentennial Grant. Today, the railway operates on weekends and in school holidays using steam engines and vintage diesel motors.

There is a delightful irony in the Great Zig Zag's rebirth. John Whitton's ghost, I suspect, might express his blunt Yorkshire disapproval at the fact that the line now runs on the narrow 3-foot 6-inch gauge he so detested, and uses vintage Queensland rolling stock.

The Great Zig Zag was regarded as one of the engineering wonders of the nineteenth century. A by-product of its construction was the development of locomotive boilers that could cope with steep grades. This, along with Whitton's other engineering innovations and construction techniques, made it possible for mountain railways to be built all over the world. Mountain railways everywhere are, to some extent, the legacy of this remarkable Yorkshireman.

Whitton has been called 'the father of the New South Wales Railways'. On his arrival on these shores in 1856 there were just 20 miles of track; when he retired in 1890, there were 2200 miles of railways in New South Wales. But, more than the size of the state's rail network, he gave the extremely lucky colony of New South Wales a system built on sensible ideas, good engineering practice and a minimum of political and economic interference and corruption.

'There were some spectacular, though relatively harmless, accidents.' NSW SA

The fact that he gave up a promising career in his native land, where railways had been in existence for several decades, to take up a position at the end of the earth and attempt to build railways through what was still uncharted wilderness, tells us a lot about this dour Yorkshireman. He remained engineer-in-chief of NSW Railways for thirty-four years and chose to live out his life here in Australia.

He died in February 1898 at his house in St Leonards and was buried in St Thomas' Cemetery, North Sydney. Twenty years earlier *The Town and Country Journal* had published what could have been a fitting epitaph: 'Among the public men of the colony who occupy professional positions ... none is more distinguished for ability than Mr John Whitton, the Engineer-in-Chief of Railways, none, it may be said, is equal to the grandeur of his achievements.'

Such things are commonly said about public figures when they retire or die. It is telling that these qualities were often attributed to John Whitton during his working life.

## AN INFLUENCE BEYOND RAILWAYS?

Australia has the second oldest national park in the world (Yellowstone in the USA is the oldest). The Royal National Park, south of Sydney, was proclaimed in 1879 and it can be argued that it is in a strange way, a legacy of John Whitton's honesty. Not that he had any interest in national parks, just building railway lines well and efficiently.

Owning land through which a railway line would pass could be lucrative because the government had to resume the land and pay compensation. When the line was being surveyed south of Sydney in the early 1870s, speculation was rife and many politicians and their cronies, thinking the line would go through the Hacking River valley, bought the land that now makes up the Royal National Park.

Whitton, however, selected the Bottle Forest route along the ridges to the west and the speculators were left holding worthless land. It seems that they had enough 'friends' in the government to stop construction of the line for some months when it reached Sutherland, hoping that Whitton could be convinced to change his mind. Whitton's decision prevailed, as it usually did, and the line continued down through the Bottle Forest.

Strange to say, the 'kindly' government purchased the land anyway and saved the speculators from financial loss. Apparently it was decided that what the colony needed was something unheard of at the time — a national park.

# TO MELBOURNE BY TRAIN

*by Mark Twain (from* **Following the Equator***)*

### MARK TWAIN IN AUSTRALIA

How wonderful it is to have the greatest American humourist of the age writing about the absurdity of the different gauges used in Australia. Samuel Clements, who wrote under the pen-name of 'Mark Twain', visited Australia in 1895 as part of a world lecture tour. He was, of course, the most famous humourist, author and speaker of his day.

His health was not good at the time but he was forced to do the tour as he needed the money rather desperately. Twain had lost his entire fortune when his publishing company made an ill-advised investment in a new printing venture. But while the tour was an unfortunate necessity for Twain, it was a stroke of luck for us. Without Twain's impending bankruptcy, we would never had had this wonderful writer observing and recording his impressions of Australian life.

He had quite a bit to say about Australian railways and railway towns, including the wry observation that 'The local Railway Station of any town worth its salt, and with any sort of pretensions, was up there architecturally with the Town Hall, church, court house and maybe the better class of licensed establishment.' Over fifty years after the lecture tour, having reported Twain's comments on the town when he visited Victoria, *The Maryborough Advertiser* would remind its readers:

*Mark Twain is credited with designating the town as 'a railway station with a town attached'. The designation has frequently been quoted, both in terms of criticism and praise. After all we would not be stretching the imagination so far as our railway station is concerned, because it is a structure which still stands as a monument to its builders and gives the town more than ordinary distinction.*

Perhaps Twain's observations on the importance of a town's railway station are some indication of just how vital the railways were to the whole development of our nation. It has always seemed that railways played a very particular role in Australia's history because their development almost exactly paralleled the economic growth of Australia.

Like most of Twain's writing, the piece that follows just oozes quotable quotes. He sums up the whole business of the colonies choosing different gauges as perhaps only Mark Twain could: 'Think of the paralysis of intellect that gave that idea birth; imagine the boulder it emerged from on some petrified legislator's shoulders.'

For a gem such as that, and bearing in mind that Twain spent only a short time in Australia, we should forgive the small inaccuracies in this piece of writing. Yes, he appears to misplace the Blue Mountains by several hundred miles and confuses sheep dip with shearers' tar, but then many city-dwelling Australians wouldn't know the difference between sheep dip and shearers' tar, either.

My health had broken down in Sydney, but not until after I had had a good outing, and had also filled my lecture engagements. This latest break lost me the chance of seeing Queensland. In the circumstances, to go north toward hotter weather was not advisable.

So we moved south with a westward slant, 17 hours by rail to the capital of the colony of Victoria, Melbourne – that juvenile city of 60 years, and half a million inhabitants. On the map the distance looked small; but that is a trouble with all divisions of distance in such a vast country as Australia. The colony of Victoria itself looks small on the map – looks like a county, in fact – yet it is about as large as England, Scotland, and Wales combined. Or, to get another focus upon it, it is just 80 times as large as the state of Rhode Island, and one-third as large as the state of Texas.

Outside of Melbourne, Victoria seems to be owned by a handful of squatters, each with a Rhode Island for a sheep farm. That is the impression which one gathers from common talk, yet the wool industry of Victoria is by no means so great as that of New South Wales. The climate of Victoria is favourable to many great industries – among others, wheat growing and the making of wine.

We took the train from Sydney at about four in the afternoon. It was American in one way, for we had a most rational sleeping car; also the car was clean and fine and new – nothing about it to suggest the rolling stock of the continent of Europe. But our baggage was weighed, and extra weight charged for. That was continental. Continental and troublesome. Any detail of railroading that is not troublesome cannot honourably be described as continental.

The tickets were round-trip ones – to Melbourne, and clear to Adelaide in South Australia, and then all the way back to Sydney. Twelve hundred more miles than we really expected to make; but then as the round trip wouldn't cost much more than the single trip, it seemed well enough to buy as many miles as one could afford, even if one was not likely to need them. A human being has a natural desire to have more of a good thing than he needs.

Now comes a singular thing: the oddest thing, the strangest thing, the most baffling and unaccountable marvel that Australasia can show. At the frontier between New South Wales and Victoria our multitude of passengers were routed out of their snug beds by lantern-light in the morning in the biting cold of a high altitude to change cars on a road that has no break in it from Sydney to Melbourne! Think of the paralysis of intellect that gave that idea birth; imagine the boulder it emerged from on some petrified legislator's shoulders.

It is a narrow-gauge road to the frontier, and a broader gauge thence to Melbourne. The two governments were the builders of the road and are the owners of it. One or two reasons are given for this curious state of things. One is, that it represents the jealousy existing between the colonies – the two most important colonies of Australasia. What the other one is, I have forgotten. But it is of no consequence. It could be but another effort to explain the inexplicable.

All passengers fret at the double-gauge; all shippers of freight must of course fret at it; unnecessary expense, delay, and annoyance are imposed upon everybody concerned, and no one is benefited.

Each Australian colony fences itself off from its neighbour with a customhouse. Personally, I have no objection, but it must be a good deal of inconvenience to the people. We have something resembling it here and there in America, but it goes by another name. The large empire of the Pacific coast requires a world of iron machinery, and could manufacture it economically on the spot if the imposts on foreign iron were removed. But they are not. Protection to Pennsylvania and Alabama forbids it. The result to the Pacific coast is the same as if there were several rows of custom-fences between the coast and the East. Iron carted across the American continent at luxurious railway rates would be valuable enough to be coined when it arrived.

We changed cars. This was at Albury. And it was there, I think, that the growing day and the early sun exposed the distant range called the Blue Mountains. Accurately named. 'My word!' as the Australians say, but it was a stunning colour, that blue. Deep, strong, rich, exquisite; towering and majestic masses of blue – a softly luminous blue, a smouldering blue, as if vaguely lit by fires within. It extinguished the blue of the sky – made it pallid and unwholesome, whitey and washed-out. A wonderful colour – just divine.

A resident told me that those were not mountains; he said they were rabbit-piles. And explained that long exposure and the over-ripe condition of the rabbits was what made them look so blue. This man may have been right, but much reading of books of travel has made me distrustful of gratis information furnished by unofficial residents of a country. The facts which such people give to travellers are usually erroneous, and often intemperately so. The rabbit-plague has indeed been very bad in Australia, and it could account for one mountain, but not for a mountain range, it seems to me. It is too large an order.

We breakfasted at the station. A good breakfast, except for the coffee; and cheap. The Government establishes the prices and placards them. The waiters were men, I think; but that is not usual in Australasia. The usual thing is to have girls. No, not girls, young ladies – generally duchesses. Dress? They would attract attention at any royal levee in Europe. Even empresses and queens do not dress as they do. Not that they could not afford it, perhaps, but they would not know how.

All the pleasant morning we slide smoothly along over the plains, through thin – not thick – forests of great melancholy gum trees, with trunks rugged with curled sheets of flaking bark – erysipelas convalescents, so to speak, shedding their dead skins. And all along were tiny cabins built sometimes of wood, sometimes of grey-blue corrugated iron; and the doorsteps and fences were clogged with children – rugged little simply clad chaps that looked as if they had been imported from the banks of the Mississippi without breaking bulk.

'We took the train from Sydney at about four in the afternoon.' NSW SA

Albury Railway Station at the time of Twain's visit. 'The local railway station was up there architecturally with the Town Hall.' NSW SA

And there were little villages, with neat stations well placarded with showy advertisements – mainly of almost *too* self-righteous brands of 'sheep-dip'. If that is the name – and I think it is. It is a stuff like tar, and is dabbed on to places where the shearer clips a piece out of the sheep. It bars out the flies, and has healing properties, and a nip to it, which makes the sheep skip like the cattle on a thousand hills. It is not good to eat. That is, it is not good to eat except when mixed with railroad coffee. It improves railroad coffee. Without it railroad coffee is too vague. But with it, it is quite assertive and enthusiastic. By itself, railroad coffee is too passive, but sheep-dip makes it wake up and get down to business. I wonder where they get railroad coffee?

We saw birds, but not a kangaroo, not an emu, not an ornithorhynchus, not a lecturer, not a native. Indeed, the land seemed quite destitute of game. But I have misused the word native. In Australia it is applied to Australian-born whites only. I should have said that we saw no Aboriginals – no 'blackfellows'. And to this day I have never seen one. In the great museums you will find all the other curiosities, but in the curio of chiefest interest to the stranger, all of them are lacking. We have at home an abundance of museums, and not an American Indian in them. It is clearly an absurdity, but it never struck me before.

# TO THE CITY

*by Steele Rudd (adapted from* On an Australian Farm*)*

## THE TRIALS OF TRAVEL

A warm and glorious sunshine lit up the land. The fields of waving wheat breaking into shot-blade were pictures good for man to see. The great pine trees towering round the snuggling home were a-song with birds and all the family were up to their eyes with the final preparations for the trip to the city.

For a week and more Mrs Dashwood and the girls had been overhauling and organising their wardrobes, and packing boxes and bags and portmanteaux, so that no hitch would happen and no time be lost when the hour for starting arrived. Tilly, who had had more experience in travelling than the others, was careful to send Maria, her married sister, instructions to do likewise, and warned her to leave nothing to the last. And Maria sent a message to say that she and the baby were ready to start at any moment.

Preparations for a church picnic, or for attending a race meeting, are exciting enough events in the country, but this trip to the city excelled all things in the history of 'Fairfield'. Nothing had ever so disorganised and dislocated the family nerve and general placidity.

There is no class on earth so easily and speedily demoralised as the country person when under the spell and influence of a 'trip to the city'. But the demoralisation lasts only until their feet touch the floor of the railway carriage, and they feel the grip of the ticket and the carriage window. Then, with a gulp and a gasp, the temporary disorder passes away like the evil effects of green lucerne leaving a bloated cow when proper remedies are applied.

Old John, arrayed in a shining black suit with a heavy gold chain stretched across his great stomach, strutted into the dining room and surveyed himself in a self-satisfied sort of way. A big man was old John, and done up and posing as he was now, looked all over a prosperous alderman.

Granny in a motherly way looked him up and down, then took him in charge and tugged at the sleeves and tails of his coat to coax them into position. Then, taking out her pocket-handkerchief, she proceeded to brush him all over.

Peter, dressed like a shop window, in a loud check suit, a cunning-looking tweed hat – the only one of its kind in the land – a high-coloured collar, a variegated necktie, and carrying a spanking new leather bag in each hand, skipped breezily into the room.

For a moment John's breath threatened to leave him. He stared long and hard at his artistic-looking son. Peter paraded the room as if for inspection. Old John started to smile.

'Well,' said old John, 'if I wouldn't a'thought you was just come back from heaven.'

'By Jove, then, Father,' Peter rejoined enthusiastically, 'you don't look too bad yourself. You'd pass for a king in those clothes.'

James, carelessly dressed in a common tweed suit, and wearing a soft felt hat, sauntered in search of luggage to convey to the buggies standing in the yard. His eyes rested on Peter and he stopped abruptly, and stared.

Old John, looking at James, said, 'Don't you know him, lad? Did you think he were the Dook o' York?'

James burst into merriment and, turning on his heel, retreated down the corridor. The next moment he was heard calling to the girls.

'What is it, James?' Tilly answered. 'We'll be ready now in a moment.'

'For heaven's sake,' James said, 'just go and look in at the dining room!'

Neither Tilly nor Polly could resist curiosity. Clad in their sombre travelling dresses they hurried to the dining room and looked in curiously and expectantly. For a second or two they experienced only disappointment, for their eyes rested only on the forms of Granny and old John. When, however, the gorgeous and smiling figure of Peter standing rigid and erect took shape to them, they simultaneously shrieked and fled.

'They be a'laughin' at you, lad,' old John remarked with a grin at Peter.

'Those who laugh last, Father, laugh longest,' Peter said. 'Wait till we get to the city, and see who'll be laughed at then, not me. Ha, ha, ha!'

Mrs Dashwood and Maria and the baby assembled in the dining room and dumped a consignment of small luggage on the table.

'Did anyone see Maria's basket?' Mrs Dashwood asked.

But Maria, herself, stifled a reply. 'Oh *Peter*!' she exclaimed on beholding her brother. Then she started to laugh.

'Well, I'm blowed if I know what you all see wrong about me to laugh at,' Peter protested. And once more he stepped out round the room in a gallant parade.

'Really,' Maria said advisedly, 'you don't show a bit of taste, Peter, not a bit.'

'Don't show a bit of *taste*?' Peter echoed. 'There's a good joke in there somewhere, Father, but I'm blessed if I can get it off my tongue.'

James, who had returned quietly to the room, started to grin. 'If there's a better joke there than himself,' he remarked slyly to Maria, 'I'll be very much surprised.'

William appeared, and announced that everything was ready and advised them to get a move on.

Polly and Tilly, with their hats in their hands, paid final visits to the mirror. Granny put up a hue and cry about the loss of one of her woollen 'mitts' that all the while was in her pocket, and started the others off on a wild goose chase.

'Now then, for the city,' Peter cried, lifting his hand and adjusting his quaint little hat.

'Oh, wait just a minute!' Polly exclaimed excitedly. 'What on earth did I do with my umbrella?'

'Clad in their sombre travelling dresses …' BCC

They turned the place upside down in search of the umbrella and eventually discovered that Granny was nursing it all the while.

Out in the sun Polly and Tilly tittered and said, 'Just look at Peter!'

Then they clamoured and climbed into the four-wheeler. James opened and closed the big white gate. The whip cracked and away they rolled to the railway station.

A sharp twenty minutes' drive past McFlaherty's farm, around Catherton's corner, and they reached the station.

The bulk of the luggage, which had preceded them on Smith's wagon, occupied a whole end of the platform. The stationmaster and his porter were busy engaged disfiguring it all with labels.

The stationmaster raised his cap to the ladies, all of whom smiled graciously upon him, and passed pleasant remarks to old John on his appearance and expressed envy at his freedom and prospects of a good time in the city.

'Ahh, I be goin' to enjoy meself, Johnson,' old John assured him. 'It be the first trip we've taken and we're a'goin' to do it in style.'

'I don't blame you,' the stationmaster said. 'Peter looks like he is going to have a good time, Mr Dashwood.'

With a 'Ha, ha, ha!' Peter spun around three times on one heel.

'Ahh,' said old John with a smile, 'Peter thinks he is a'going to take the city by storm.'

'I don't know about taking the city by storm,' the cheerful stationmaster answered, 'but he might take some of the city girls by storm.'

'Ha, ha, ha!' and Peter made several revolutions on his other heel.

The stationmaster, glancing towards the ladies to see they were not within hearing, placed his mouth close to old John's ear and said something confidential.

'Hoh, hoh, hoh! I don't think he would go *thet* far!' old John roared.

'Then he's a lot different to what his father was at his age, I bet,' the stationmaster replied.

Old John broke into another loud, 'Hoh, hoh, hoh!'. 'Look here Johnson,' he laughed, 'I'll have you dismissed at headquarters, when I gets to the city.'

Meanwhile Mrs Dashwood and Maria and the girls were busy swapping and changing and arranging the smaller items of luggage. Polly required a certain bag taken into the carriage and Tilly a particular box, while Mrs Dashwood and Maria expressed grave doubts as to the safety of a trunk in the van.

'All travelling "first", Mr Dashwood?' the stationmaster inquired, as he procured the tickets.

'Aye, all first,' old John answered, taking out his purse.

'What about Peter?' the official smiled significantly.

'Peter?' answered old John, turning and eyeing the magnificently dressed one. 'Ahh, but now you haven't anythin' better 'n "first" have you Johnson?'

'Not here,' the other answered, prodding the tickets into the date stamp. 'But I dare say we could get the Governor's carriage if we wired right away.'

'Ha, ha, ha!' Peter went off. 'I'd look as well in it as old thing-a-me-bob the Lieutenant Governor.'

'You'd look a jolly sight better, if you ask me,' the stationmaster broke into a chuckle.

'He'd look better in the dog-box,' James drawled, gazing out at the railway yard.

Just then the mail whistled and a scramble set in.

'That's her!' the stationmaster cried.

Old John and James and Peter snapped up articles of luggage. William kissed Maria and the baby and said 'goodbye' to the others.

The train drew up to the platform and one after the other the family crowded noisily into it, much to the annoyance of two 'commercials', who lay full stretch on the seats. The stationmaster banged the door noisily after them, then stood on the carriage step and wished them all a good time and a safe return. Old John and James waved to those on the platform. The train whistled and puffed, strained, and went off.

## ON THE TRAIN

The train in full motion tore along on her course, rattling and roaring over bridges and culverts. Calico tents, camps, navvies' homes, mountains, and timber lands were flung one upon another, and at every gate and every siding a whirlpool of dust and dead leaves rose in her wake.

'By Jove, this is all right, eh, Father?' Peter, standing with a firm grip of the carriage window, shouted joyfully.

Mrs Dashwood began to exhibit symptoms of fear. 'I hope nothing goes wrong!' she cried nervously.

'Ha! Ha! Ha!' Peter yelled. 'Mother thinks we'll go off the line!'

'It might then,' said old John, smiling blandly in the corner that he had appropriated to himself. 'It won't be th' first time she went off on this line.'

'Oh, Father, how could it!' from Polly.

'Of course it could go off!' Mrs Dashwood assured her daughters, her eyes widening with increased alarm.

'Well, if she does,' James remarked philosophically, 'there won't be many of us left to tell the tale.'

'Oh, oh,' came from Mrs Dashwood in gasps, as the train made a bit of a lurch.

'Ha! Ha! Ha!' from Peter.

'Ho! Ho! Ho!' laughed old John. 'Doan be frightent of a train, Eliza! Look there at Granny – she dersent mind.'

Granny, contentedly munching biscuits, and gazing out on a vast stretch of rich plain land that lay in view, looked as though she had been reared in a train.

At that moment the carriage rocked violently as she swung round a curve, and only old John and James seemed to have been prepared for it. The others thought they had reached the end of the world, and that their time had come. Several short screams escaped the women, and they clutched at each other for support and salvation.

Peter, who lost all his balance, was thrown sideways into old John's lap.

'Oh dear! Oh dear!' Mrs Dashwood moaned on realising that all was yet well. 'I thought we were gone!'

The girls and Maria, recovering, laughed hysterically at their own foolishness.

Peter gathered himself together, and with a forced 'Ha, ha, ha!' courageously took his place at the window again.

'By Jove!' he cried. 'It's great sport trying to hang on here.'

The two commercials who had exiled themselves and their belongings to the furthermost part of the carriage lay quietly smiling at all the fuss and fears of their travelling companions. Occasionally they lifted a magazine and appeared to be deeply engrossed in its contents. But they were frauds and shams, those commercials. They read not a line. They used the magazines as barricades, behind which they closely observed the actions of Polly and Tilly and the rest – but more especially Polly and Tilly. At intervals they would say things to each other and smile.

'*They* haven't seen many trains, Monty?' one said.

'The old man has seen some "brass", though,' the other answered.

'How do you like the fair one?' (meaning Tilly) the former remarked further.

'Good style, isn't she?' was the answer. They both pretended to read some more.

'Ha, ha, ha! Look, Father! Look at the coves drawing wood with a team of goats!' Peter broke out in a burst of ecstasy.

'Oh, look!' the girls echoed, and Mrs Dashwood gripped Andy by the leg to prevent him falling through the window in his eagerness to get a full view of the curiosity.

'See the goats, Granny?' Maria cried, nudging the old lady hard in the ribs.

'A boat, is it?' said Granny. 'I were in a boat one time, an' it turned right over an' –'

Granny's irrelevant discourse was cut short by the excitable Peter.

'Ha, ha, ha!' he yelled. 'Did you see the whiskers on the leader, Father? As long as an old man's.'

'I think he were an ol' man, thet cove,' the parent replied, 'be th' look on him.'

'Are they good pullers?' Peter questioned. Peter was travelling now, and bent on gathering useful information.

'Good pullers?' said old John, raising his voice to make himself heard. 'Soomtimes they be an' soomtimes they bain't.'

'Oh, they always pull,' James vouchsafed for Peter's information, 'if they're put in a good paddock.'

Peter stared wonderingly at James, and asked: 'Why in a good paddock?'

'Well,' James drawled with a grin, 'if there is good grass in it.'

Peter saw the joke, and laughed hard.

'What were that?' inquired old John, curiously.

'James said they'll pull grass, Father,' Peter shouted.

'Aye, they will thet,' said the parent, 'an' they gets their owners pulled soomtimes.'

Peter's restless eye discovered a new curiosity.

'Look at this though,' he called. 'Look here! I'm jiggered. Ha! Ha! Ha!'

The others looked hurriedly, and saw the humble homestead of a struggling selector scattered about. Three lanky youths in charge of a lean, dreary-looking horse fastened in some way to a fork-stick on which a water cask was being conveyed in the direction of the home. One of the youths was pulling the quadruped along by the rein; another was astride it wielding a big stick on its ribs; the third was engaged in the dual capacity of conductor and driver. He balanced the cask with one hand and threw stones and things at the animal with the other.

'Poor things!' Mrs Dashwood said, feelingly.

'An irrigation plant!' James drawled.

'Ha! Ha! Ha!' Peter exploded. 'Look at the bloke on the moke's back – look at him, Father! Look at him.'

Tilly was beginning to feel ashamed of Peter. Tilly felt that the eyes of those commercials were upon them, and she was inclined to be sensitive.

'Peter, don't be such a silly!' she said. 'Do you want everyone to be laughing at you?'

Polly and Maria glanced round, and discovered the two strangers half strangling themselves with suppressed mirth.

'I declare,' they said, 'those men are laughing at us!'

'No wonder!' Tilly snapped indignantly. 'The way he's going on would make a fool of anyone!'

But Peter didn't hear his sister's reprimand. His mind was all on the water carriers.

'Ha, ha!' he started again, but suddenly checked himself. Then like a crack of lightning he went off.

'Ha! Ha! Ha! Ha! Ha! Ha! It's capsized! Ha! Ha! Ha!'

There was another rush for window space. Even the placid commercials sat up and looked out.

'Surely it bain't!' said old John, sharing a window with James for a glimpse of the catastrophe.

'Poor people! What a shame!' murmured Mrs Dashwood.

But the train plunging into a deep cutting excluded everything but memories of that selection scene from view.

'That's farming under difficulties for you, if you like!' James, with a sympathetic shake of the head, remarked as he settled again in his seat.

'Ah doan know if it be farmin', lad,' old John answered. 'But I knows thet I'd sooner go to gaol than go on th' land thet way.'

'Do you think there's any excuse for that sort of thing nowadays?' James asked.

'Well,' the parent replied thoughtfully, 'not fer ridin' th' horse, I don't expect. There be a lot o' bad menagement about that lot, no doubt, but there'll allus be people fightin' up hill, lad, as long as they go on th' land wi' no capital. It takes a heap o' money – more'n people think – to take oop land an' make headway. I knows what it means. I've been through it all, an' so have your Moother. A lot of 'em think so long as they get hold on th' land they're right, whereas most times they're all wrong.'

'Well, people struggling like those we just passed,' James suggested, 'would be much better off working on wages?'

'Far an' away better off,' the parent said. 'They'd have no worry, for one thing, an' they'd have a shillin' or two to spend soomtimes.'

'I see where the Minister for Lands said the other day,' James remarked, 'that he knew of cases where men went on the land with only half-a-crown in their pocket, and became well off.'

'He sez soome queer things, do the Minister for Lands,' old John replied, 'soome very queer things! But what you never do hear 'im sayin', lad, is that his own father spent oondreds o' pounds sendin' him away to be edcrcated fer a barrister, an' that after all his edercation he couldn't make a livin' at it. He were a failure!'

'So I believe,' James said, 'and Judge Smith with scarcely any schooling made his way from the carpenter's shop to the Bench.'

'Aye, an' there you have it,' explained the parent. 'Thet were just th' difference atween he an' Judge Smith; an' so wi' men on the land. But fer all thet it dersent stand at all, lad, an' Judge Smith, I knows, would tell the same, thet the surest way to reach the Bench bain't be by neglectin' school, or startin' from a carpenter's shop!'

The roar of the locomotive now made it almost impossible to hear their own voices.

'I can't hear!' James shouted, leaning over towards his parent.

Old John leaned over, too, and bellowed out something, which sounded like a gramophone in distress.

'Just so,' James answered speculatively.

'Only a fool,' was all James caught next.

'Yes,' he ventured, nodding his head in approval, but of what he hadn't the slightest idea.

Old John gesticulated vehemently, and his eloquence seemed to increase under the disadvantages of the noise.

'... land ... No ... how could he ... seasons ... slightest chance ... all th' same,' fell from him in distorted fragments.

'I dare say,' James shouted.

Seeming satisfied with the impression his words were making, old John, using his large, leathery finger to emphasise his discourse, proceeded vigorously:

'... forty bushels ... could ... dry seasons ... horses ... settlement ... do y' think?'

Then pausing, he seemed to expect a reply.

'Oh, I think you're right,' James replied with a grin.

Old John shook his head in a dissatisfied sort of way, and wagging his finger more, repeated the observation:

'... dairying ... no man ... land ... close settlement ... could anyone ... twenty years,' he said.

'Oh, no doubt,' James yelled, with another grin.

'What?' old John roared.

James desired to end the joke, and tapped himself on the ear and shook his head.

But old John was a persistent old man, and never liked to give in – not even to the noise of a train.

'... ploughed land ... miles and miles ... their fault ... a great country ... people ... night follows day ... millions ...'

'Do you think so?' James yelled, taking up the joke again.

'What!' old John howled.

'Millions of people,' James said.

'Certainly – why not?' roared the parent.

Just then everything was thrown into darkness, and the noise increased twofold. Sharp, nervous screams came from the women, and they huddled into each other for protection, and from Peter came a loud 'Ha, ha, ha!' They were passing through a tunnel, but it seemed as though they were passing into eternity. Just as suddenly the light rushed in again, as the tunnel came to an end and heavy sighs of relief fell from Mrs Dashwood and Maria. The deafening noise had ended too, and once more they could converse freely.

Peter leaned out and stared back in astonishment at the mouth of that tunnel, while Polly and Tilly desired to know the name of it.

Maria said she 'had heard what it was called, but couldn't think of the name of it.'

'Ah-h dersent know at all,' old John candidly admitted, and supposed that it 'went by soome name or other.'

One of the commercials who had moved into a seat that brought him nearer the family, and was evincing a deeper interest in passing objects, supplied the information: 'That's the Royal tunnel,' he said, addressing old John.

Polly and Tilly stole sly glances at the sample hawker.

'Ah-h, it be the Royal tunnel,' echoed old John, for the information of his daughters.

'Oh, the Royal tunnel,' they murmured together.

'Yes, that's it,' Maria exclaimed, giving the baby a shake up, 'the Royal. I remember the name now.'

'Really, Maria!' Tilly said with a mischievous smile.

Maria went crimson. She nearly went off the handle, too; but the baby starting to cry saved the situation.

'It's the longest tunnel in the State,' the commercial further acquainted old John.

'It's the longest tunnel there be,' old John promptly informed his relations without acknowledging his source of distorted information.

'Nearly a mile long,' the other commercial, who had shifted nearer too, called out.

'Just fancy – nearly a mile long!' Mrs Dashwood said, addressing her daughters. 'It didn't seem half that.'

'Tunnels are not what they seem, Mother,' Tilly answered, playfully parodying some of the 'Psalm of Life'.

Both commercials shifted their eyes to Tilly, and one, more learned than the other, said egotistically: 'And the grave is not its goal.'

Tilly looked away and smiled.

The commercials nudged each other.

James was curious to know who the contractors were that constructed the line, and interrogated the commercials. They stared. It was out of their line.

'Contractors?' they said, with puzzled airs. 'Goodness knows.'

'Wilks, I suppose it would be?' James suggested, turning to his parent.

'Aye, I think it would be,' old John answered.

The commercial men eyed James curiously. They seemed to regard him as a waste of time. But James paid no further attention to them, and they took up their magazines and continued reading between the lines.

Polly and Tilly, however, would occasionally steal glances at the backs of the magazines, and then whisper things to each other and titter.

'Tilly!' Mrs Dashwood said sharply. 'What is the matter with you?'

'I'm amused at Granny, Mother,' Tilly answered diplomatically.

Mrs Dashwood turned and saw Granny with her head well back against the cushion, and her mouth open in deep slumber.

'Poor Granny,' she said, 'is tired out!' And taking a lace handkerchief from her pocket placed it over the aged one's face to keep the flies from disturbing her. And, with her long, lean hands hanging lifelessly beside her, Granny looked like a corpse laid out on a chair.

After passing through mile upon mile of smouldering, smoking waste lands over which a fierce bush fire had obviously been raging for many days, after flying past Mullungangerina and Niccoloconjoorooroo, and Bibleback, and Howe, and many other strange places, large suburban residences with luxuriant gardens and white paling fences about them began to show up.

A succession of small shops took shape; pedestrians and motors and bikes began to come along in numbers, and the ascending spires of lofty churches elevated on hills, and volumes of black smoke curling into the sky could be seen from the windows.

Through the last cutting the train rushed, then the great city in all its age, in all its youth, in all its glory, in all its grime, in all its grandeur and in all its dirt and dust burst full before our country friends.

Excitement! There *was* excitement! None of them could remain still a minute longer. Not even Granny, who woke up and wished to know where she was, and how long she had been asleep. They were all in a flurry.

The door flew open and a railway porter bounced in.

'Tickets, please!' he cried sharply.

'Tickets,' Polly and Tilly repeated, looking at old John.

'Ahhh,' and old John started fumbling in his pockets.

'I saw you get them from Mr Johnson, Father,' Peter remarked.

The others regarded old John with anxious eyes.

The porter regarded him as an outrage. 'Can't you find them?' he said, impatiently.

'I put 'em somewhere,' answered old John, screwing and twisting his body about to fit his big hands into his pockets.

'You surely can't have lost them, Father?' Mrs Dashwood murmured with increased anxiety.

'You haven't got them, Mother?' Tilly suggested, looking at Mrs Dashwood.

Mrs Dashwood shook her head and said she hadn't even seen them.

The official lost patience. 'I can't wait on you all night,' he snapped. 'Oh, you'll have to come to see the SM,' and opening the door commanded them to follow him to the magnate's office.

They seized their luggage and, like Brown's cows, followed him. Some of them looked solemn; some looked convicted of bigamy; some looked amused.

Tilly and Polly hid their faces with things they were carrying and tittered.

'Goodness gracious me!' Tilly said. 'What on earth will people think of us!'

The great platform along which they trailed was thronged with people. Some of them were scrambling and jostling for possession of luggage; some running up and down peering into railway carriages; some hugging long lost brothers and sisters; and a great number staring curiously at the cortege that trooped at the heels of the swaggering railway man.

Hotel porters and boarding house touts thrust their advertising cards into old John's hand, and into the hands of every member of the family, and shouted the virtues of their respective establishments into their ears.

The crowded shelves of the open book-stalls with their glaring flaring placards inviting people to purchase the 'newest wonder' in the literary line arrested the wondering gaze of our mutual friends. But the porter was in a hurry, and they were not permitted to linger and look.

They were approaching the door of the SM's office. Old John suddenly stopped.

Central Station, Brisbane, circa 1900. BCC

'Ahh, hold on,' he said with a smile.

Old John seemed to have remembered something.

'Have you found them, Father?' the family cried. With joyful expectation in their eyes.

Old John took a tobacco pouch from his pocket, out of which he slowly extracted the missing tickets.

'That be 'em,' he said, handing them to the porter.

'A very stupid place to put tickets!' the porter remarked disappointedly, as he handed back the return halves.

'Ha, ha, ha!' laughed Peter. 'You got 'em, eh, Father?'

'Oh, I knew I had 'em soomwheres,' said old John.

And they turned and departed.

# ON THE QUEENSLAND RAILWAY LINES

▬▬▬▬▬▬▬▬▬▬▬▬▬▬▬▬▬▬▬▬▬▬▬▬▬▬▬▬▬▬▬▬▬▬▬▬▬▬▬▬▬

*Anon*

> *On the Queensland railway lines*
> *There are stations where one dines;*
> *Private individuals*
> *Also run refreshment stalls.*
> *Pies and coffee, baths and showers*
> *Are supplied at Charters Towers;*
> *At Mackay the rule prevails*
> *Of restricting showers to males.*
>
> *Bogan-Tungan, Rollingstone,*
> *Mungar, Murgon, Marathon*
> *Guthalungra, Pinkenba,*
> *Wanko, Yaamba — ha, ha, ha!*
>
> *Males and females, high and dry,*
> *Hang around at Durikai,*
> *Boora-Mugga, Djarawong,*
> *Giligulgul, Wonglepong.*

'On a Queensland railway line.' Two view of Rollingstone Station. TCL *(both pics)*

*Iron rations come in handy*
*On the way to Dirranbandi;*
*Passengers have died of hunger*
*During halts at Garradunga.*

*Bogan-Tungan, Rollingstone,*
*Mungar, Murgon, Marathon*
*Guthalungra, Pinkenba,*
*Wanko, Yaamba – ha, ha, ha!*

*Let us toast, before we part,*
*Those who travel, stout of heart,*
*Drunk or sober, rain or shine,*
*On a Queensland railway line.*

# NOT AT THE STATION

*by Russell Hannah & Jim Haynes*

'Gee, the railways are getting some pretty bad press lately,' I said to Leo the Lover as I joined him at his table. 'I read in the paper where a woman complained about a bloke relieving himself between the carriages on a night train she was on. She reckoned he should have held on to it and got off at the next station. She tried to have him arrested.'

'I got caught like that once,' said Leo the Lover. 'I got off at the station and had to wait three hours for the next train. And the worst part was, when I got off, the dunny was locked anyway.'

'I s'pose you'd had a few beers,' I said to Leo, just to put it into perspective.

'Not on your life,' he replied. 'In fact I'd had a touch of blood pressure and had to take a diuretic, and you know what they do to you.'

'I know what they did to Shane Warne. He got banned for twelve months for telling a story like that. I hope your mother didn't give it to you.'

Leo ignored my comment. 'You know,' he said, 'in the early days, trains didn't have toilets for the passengers, not even country trains, but that was before my time.'

'Before my time too. But I remember the WCs in those old dogbox and side-corridor carriages. You know, the ones that used to drop straight onto the track. The ones you weren't allowed to use while the train was standing at the station.'

'Ha!' said Leo. 'I bet you don't remember the song about them.'

At this point Leo burst into song, which naturally attracted the attention of Cranky Cec, the barman.

Cec wasn't that fond of Leo the Lover. Leo sometimes stayed on a bit late and demanded drinks after closing time in a manner that Cec found offensive. Also, singing in the club is regarded as a disturbance to other patrons and is often taken as a sign of intoxication. It can even result in the barman refusing to serve you a drink, particularly if the barman's Cranky Cec.

But, as it was still early in the night and there seemed to be little question of Leo's sobriety, Cec bit his tongue and turned his attention to other patrons.

This is what Leo sang:

*Passengers will please refrain,*
*From using toilet while the train,*
*Is standing at the station for a while.*
*We encourage constipation,*
*While the train is at the station,*
*Passengers please hold it for a while.*

As Leo was singing, Henry the Hun, who had been ordering a beer, joined us at the table.

Henry listened intently as Leo finished his song, and then sipped his beer and claimed that Leo had the tune wrong.

'Your singing's appalling, Leo,' he remarked casually. 'That's supposed to go to the tune of a classical piece of music called "Humoresque".'

Henry fancies himself as a bit of a classical music buff, perhaps because of his Germanic origin. He has actually heard of such people as Wagner, Strauss, Chopin and Beethoven, though he's a bit vague on what they composed.

'I remember when I was a kid,' I said, 'we used to sing that whenever we went on a train. It was written on a little brass plate near the toilets.'

'Only the first bit of it,' Henry reminded me.

'Yeah, I know,' I replied with a laugh. 'But, you know, for years I used to duck for cover every time a plane flew overhead. I'd never travelled in a plane, but I knew about trains. It seemed to me that if planes used the same disposal system, it was best to be careful. Underneath a plane was no place to be for a young lad.'

All this time another bloke who often drinks at our table had been listening closely to the conversation. This bloke is known as Backhoe Bill. I suppose Backhoe Bill is known as Backhoe Bill because he once drove a backhoe. He had also spent many years working as a contractor to the railways. He used to clear the scrub away from the side of the line, repair drainage channels and assist in the replacement of sleepers. Normally Backhoe Bill doesn't say much, but talk of railways gets him quite animated and loquacious at times.

'You know,' said Backhoe, 'when they took those carriages with the long-drop dunnies out of service it was a sad day for us old track workers.'

'Why was that, Backhoe?' asked Henry. 'It would have solved the problem of putting your foot in it, so to speak.'

'Well, a lot of us track workers were keen gardeners in those days,' Backhoe told him. As he spoke his eyes took on a misty glaze and his mind seemed to drift back to the halcyon days that he spent behind his machine. 'No one went to the nursery then to get their vegie and flower seedlings. We grew them all from the seed from last year's crop.'

'You won't be able to do that once they patent the genetically modified crops,' interrupted Leo, who likes to toss in a diversion to stuff up anyone's story but his own.

Backhoe Bill ignored Leo. He was intent on finishing his tale. 'It was the tomatoes,' he said. 'We'd walk along the line during early spring and look for young tomato seedlings. Even though you knew what they'd be growing out of and where they came from, they were the biggest, tastiest, strongest tomatoes you could ever grow and eat. I suppose it was because they had a really good start in life.

'We used to call them "ring tomatoes". Gee, they were beaut, but they disappeared when they put the dunnies with container tanks into the trains.'

'Progress does have its drawbacks,' remarked Leo profoundly.

The nostalgic silence that followed was broken, as it often was, by Henry the Hun.

'My Great Uncle Claude,' said Henry, reflectively, 'was a stationmaster on the Queensland railways for most of his life.'

I sensed a story. 'Whereabouts, Henry?' I asked.

'Well,' he continued, 'for a number of years he was in charge of a small station at a little place called Dunwinnie.'

'It must be a little place,' remarked Leo. 'I've never heard of it.'

'Well, it certainly existed in Uncle Claude's time,' said Henry, emphatically. 'Though I must admit, Dunwinnie had only one thing going for it – it was a place where engines stopped to take on water and coal. It was at the base of the range, where larger and heavier trains took on a tandem loco to help them up the steeper grades. Which meant, of course, that there was a significant period of stopping time at Dunwinnie.

'In those days there were no electric lights on the platform and no gas either. So, one of the stationmasters' jobs was to let the passengers know what station they were at.

'They did this by walking up and down the platform waving a lantern and calling out the name of the station. Sort of like a human intercom system.

'At eleven o'clock each night the overnight mail train used to make a regular stop at Dunwinnie. It stopped for about twenty-five minutes while the necessary coaling, engine changing and watering was done.

'My Great Uncle Claude used to stroll along the platform waving his lantern and calling out, "Dunwinnie, Dunwinnie, Dunwinnie!" in a loud voice. He'd do this a couple of times on the train's arrival, and again before departure.

'One particular night he was following his usual procedure when a window flew up and an angry-looking woman poked her head out. Now, the head wasn't poking out of just an ordinary window; it was one of those with frosted glass. It was the train dunny window.

'This woman was as cranky as a bagful of tiger snakes, old Great Uncle Claude reckoned. She leaned out and she yelled at the poor old bugger,' Henry laughed. 'And you'll never guess what she said!'

Henry the Hun has a sense of the dramatic and likes to get his timing right before delivering his punchlines.

'Well, unless you'd like to share the joke, I guess we never will bloody know,' growled Leo the Lover.

'Well,' chuckled Henry, determined to annoy Leo as much as possible before finishing his yarn, 'she glares at old Uncle Claude in the lantern light and says, "No! I'm not done! And how did you know my name was Winnie?"'

'I fancy there's a fair element of untruthfulness in that story,' said Leo, 'and, if you're done, Henry, it's your shout …'

*Above:* 'It was written on a little brass plate near the toilets.' RH

*Right:* When drop dunnies were replaced, emptying the posh new WCs was a job for a man in a tie. NSW SA

# THE RAILWAY HOTEL

*by Wilbur Howcroft*

*When Joe was a young 'un, his cheeks flecked with down,*
*He drew his first pay cheque to head into town.*
*Then up spoke his father, 'Son, heed my words well,*
*Keep clear of the girls at the Railway Hotel.*

*'Those harpies will fleece you of all that you own,*
*They're wicked and wanton with hearts hard as stone.*
*Believe me, young fella, the road straight to Hell*
*Begins at the door of the Railway Hotel.*

*'They'll ply you with whisky, with beer, and with gin,*
*Then, when you're half-sozzled, they'll lead you to sin.*
*They're skilled at seduction, at that they excel,*
*Those trollops who tempt at the Railway Hotel.'*

*'Gee whiz,' cried our hero, with awe on his face,*
*'So that's what goes on in that old wooden place!*
*Our parson has warned me of women who dwell*
*In dens of ill-fame, like the Railway Hotel.*

'The road straight to Hell begins at the door of the Railway Hotel.' NTL NTGP

*'It seems I can still hear that old preacher's words*
*On drinking and gambling, bad language and birds.*
*But, where did he gain such vast knowledge, pray tell,*
*Of girls like the ones at the Railway Hotel?'*

*Joe saddled his pony and girthed it up tight,*
*Then, bidding his father a hasty good night,*
*He sprang in the saddle and galloped pell-mell*
*For his destination – the Railway Hotel!*

# THE NEVER NEVER RAILWAY LINE

*by Jim Haynes*

The Northern Territory is renowned for its characters. Territorians reckon it is more 'Australian' than the rest of Australia. So, when it comes to trains, it's no surprise to find that Territory trains have always had their own uniquely 'Territorian', and very Australian, character.

The most famous Territory train is, of course, 'the Ghan', although the old Ghan was technically a South Australian train, running as it did from Port Augusta to Alice Springs. Still, the old Ghan was one of the Territory's best-known characters and icons. The old Ghan first ran in 1878, but the line didn't extend to Alice Springs until 1929. When it stopped running in 1980 it was the source of a thousand wonderful yarns and legends. The new Ghan is part of the national rail system and now links Adelaide to Darwin.

The Northern Territory's 'other' train — in fact the only other Territory train for many years — was the one that ran from Darwin down to Pine Creek. As you would expect, this train also had a unique Territory character. In *We of the Never Never*, Jeannie Gunn described it as 'a delightful train — just a simple-hearted, chivalrous, weather-beaten old bush-whacker, at the service of the entire Territory'.

Her account of her very first journey on the train is one of the highlights of that famous book. She likened the train to a large friendly prehistoric creature: 'There were no fences to shut us in; and as the train zigzagged through jungle and forest and river-valley – stopping now and then to drink deeply at magnificent rivers ablaze with water-lilies – it almost seemed as though it were some kindly Mammoth creature, wandering at will through the bush ...' Other accounts of travelling from Darwin on 'the Never Never Line' seem to suggest that the train was not, perhaps, as tame a creature as Jeannie Gunn would have us believe.

The Palmerston and Pine Creek Railway Bill was passed in 1883 and the line opened in 1888. Thousands of Chinese and Indians provided the labour. Chinese outnumbered Europeans for many years in the Northern Territory, in fact, and were essential to early development.

The line was built to take freight but rarely ran at a profit. The gold rush ended, the cattle industry was struggling, cattle stations were too far from the line and the wet season caused derailments and washaways. To top it all off, termites ate the sleepers and, in 1897, a cyclone caused massive damage that virtually closed the line for two years.

In 1912 Darwin's non-Aboriginal population was only 3310, made

'A delightful train – just a simple-hearted, chivalrous, weather-beaten old bush-whacker.' NTL MISC

up of 1418 Europeans, 1331 Chinese, 280 Aborigines of mixed race and 281 'others' – so the railway wasn't exactly busy. At the end of World War I, work began on extending the line to Emungalen, on the banks of the Katherine River. This was so that Vestey's could get its cattle to the Darwin meat works. As labour was short, Greeks, Russians and even Patagonian migrants were brought in. Many settled in the Territory to add to the Territory's melting pot.

The wildness of railway gangs in Katherine was legendary. One gang of thieves, rumoured to be railway workers, built a spur track into the bush, removed the goods in two vans, set the vans alight and covered their tracks by removing the rails.

A newspaper account from 1920, in *The Northern Territory Times and Gazette*, describes a typical trip to Pine Creek. The train was made up of a loco, two passenger carriages and ten goods cars. There were only twenty-two passengers – 'the Territory's usual mixed assortment of Britishers, Greeks, Italians, Russians, Swiss, Swedes, Half-castes and Chinese'. The reporter further describes the scene in the carriages: 'every mother's son had a bottle or a case of grog. "Ave a drink" was the password and no one declined – it wasn't manners and it was the only way to avoid arguments.' Apparently, not one bottle was left when the train pulled into Pine Creek after the nine-and-a-half-hour journey of 146 miles.

At one point, while the train was stopped at a remote station, a fight broke out between two drinkers:

> As the two combatants worked from the original scene of the action to other parts of the carriage, occupants shifted out onto the platform at the rear or onto the footboard to give them more room. The guard coming along for tickets spoilt the show by promising to throw out the grog unless there was an improvement in prevailing conditions. All hands then had a drink and declared that the guard wasn't a bad sort of poor bastard.

Another, far better behaved couple of passengers were Lord and Lady Aspley, who emigrated in the early 1920s to take up land in Western

Australia. They took the opportunity to see most of the continent and travelled wherever they could. Having spent some time in Darwin, the Aspleys decided to sample the delights of the Northern Railway, which by then had extended to the banks of the Katherine River. Their account of the journey, published a few years later in *The Amateur Settlers*, is a wonderful insight into Territory life at the time:

*This is the only one railway line in the whole of northern Australia; an area twenty-seven times the size of England. It wanders 240 miles across the continent in the direction of Adelaide, and it is believed that some day the 2000 miles gap intervening between South Australia will be bridged by the continuation of this light single-track railway to meet lines coming up from the south.*

*It was one of the conditions, when the Northern Territory was handed over to the control of the Federal Government by South Australia, that this line should be completed.*

*The train runs at infrequent intervals on a single line, and has the boast of never leaving a passenger behind. It is a friendly little affair and stops at every little wayside hut, so one may get out to look for gold quartz or flowers along the track, knowing that if the train starts without you, it will be more fussed than you are, and come back to pick you up!*

*It also holds the proud record of never having run to time, and of once attaining the extraordinary speed of 40 miles per hour after a race-meeting dinner! The engine has somewhat the appearance of the early locomotives in old prints, and displays over its driving wheel a birth certificate of 1875.*

*The first part of the journey inland was through close-growing Bush and thin jungle, where it is believed certain tropical fruits, cotton, tea, rice, coffee, and even sugar and rubber might be grown. Some experts have declared that the climate is not humid enough for rubber, others that the soil is the wrong kind for sugar, but in Australia science so often adapts conditions to prove 'the expert' wrong.*

*Romance does live in Australia, and part of the charm of travelling through the undeveloped part of the country is to see it with the magic*

'Pine Creek – where the train stops at the end of the day.' NTL NTGP

*eyes of the 'maybe-one-day'. In the meanwhile, one may note that the railway track laid by imported Chinese labour cost a shilling a yard, and fifteen shillings a yard when continued by white labour.*

*Labour is scarce and dear in the Territory and experiments are often costly failures, so at present there is nothing to see from the train between Darwin and Pine Creek – where the train stops at the end of the day – but dense, small Bush timber stretching relentlessly flat on either hand, with here and there a little clearing where some brave soul is trying to make a living. It was hot and dusty, but with pleasant company all the way it was an agreeable journey, and, we thought, much more comfortable than travelling in Java.*

*We spent the night at Pine Creek, a tiny place boasting a stationmaster, a policeman, an hotel, a store, and one or two other residents, with a few prospectors and miners searching for a lost vein of gold in the surrounding hills. There used to be a comparatively large amount of gold found around Pine Creek, but that which was easily found has long since gone. Gold is still picked up in small quantities. We saw quite a large nugget before we left Darwin.*

*Many stories linger of the gold days: the lucky prospector who was so flush that he even had his horse's shoes made of gold, and of his friend who wore gold spurs (these two gentleman seemed to have travelled all the Australian gold-fields!).*

*The following morning we went on by the same train to Emungalen – the end of the railway – where a bridge is being constructed over the Katherine River, which is nearing completion and will carry the railway on southwards. It is a tiny place with the usual store and hotel as its only public buildings.*

*Here I might say a certain amount of heavy drinking goes on. The bushman has to drink to break the monotony, and it is his only form of amusement, but on our arrival a fiat went forth by common consent that all drunkards were to 'knock off' for the week we were in the neighbourhood! The kind thought was rather pathetic, and we did not hear of it till weeks after. It showed how much women are wanted in the Northern Territory.*

'The train runs at infrequent intervals and has the boast of never leaving a passenger behind.' NTL FPPV

'World War II meant moving troops to the north.' The Ghan carries men north. NTL JM

The bridge was finally built across the Katherine River and the first train crossed in 1926. Emungalen then closed and the town of Katherine grew on the new site across the river. The line was meant to continue on to Daly Waters but, when funds ran out in the Depression, it stopped at Birdum, some 320 miles from Darwin. There was absolutely nothing at Birdum – except a buffer to indicate the end of the line.

World War II meant moving troops to the north and Darwin became a strategic defence post after the Japanese bombing raid that killed over 200 people. Shipping wasn't safe and there were 120 000 troops in Darwin, so the railway was essential for supplies. The rolling stock had been run down badly by then and the first troops arrived in converted cattle trucks. Soldiers from the eastern states evidently named the train 'Spirit of Protest' in a sarcastic parody of the modern Sydney to Melbourne 'Spirit of Progress'.

Plans were made to extend the railway from Birdum to Alice

Springs. Instead of this, however, the Stuart Highway was sealed between Alice Springs and Darwin.

After the war, despite the introduction of diesel hydraulic rail cars with air-conditioning, the line was not well patronised. It deteriorated until its closure in 1976 following damage from Cyclone Tracy two years before and frequent flooding. The rails were sold off (at $50 a ton) to Taiwan and the Philippines, and the sleepers were donated to Indonesia under the Colombo Plan.

Many Darwin people mourned the loss of their Never Never Line, as historian James Harvey noted: 'Its trains had run whenever asked, despite enemy bombs, cyclones, floods, economic depressions and recessions, government and public indifference, and the inexorable delays caused by the tropical environment.'

It's an irony that the Never Never Line has now disappeared into Australian history and folklore. You see, while that great little line no longer exists, the long-promised Adelaide to Darwin Railway, first mooted in 1858 and so long a part of Aussie folklore, is now a reality. The new Ghan ran from Adelaide to Darwin for the first time in February 2004.

'Many Darwin people mourned the loss of their Never Never Line.' NTL R

# CLEAR LINE FOR SAMMY

*by Morrie Burchill*

With his odd loping walk and peculiar dress he was a familiar sight in town. He was known as Sammy. I don't think anyone knew his second name. Everybody would say, 'Good-day Sammy,' as he passed by.

Only a favoured few would be acknowledged, with an uncontrolled sweeping wave of the arm. Invariably Sammy was dressed in a woman's overcoat. It reached past his knees and had large wide lapels. It had the remains of fur around the collar and was secured by a wide leather belt.

He always wore the same cap. It was an old railway cap with a shiny peak and it sat down on top of his ears.

Promptly at six o'clock each evening he would come up over the hill into town. He would stop opposite the post office. From his pocket he would take one of those big old-fashioned railway watches and check it against the post office clock.

Satisfied, he would then set off for the railway station.

You see Sammy was unofficial checker of the daily mail train. The railway workers had sort of adopted him. On payday when the pay car came in, Sammy would line up with the porters and fettlers to get his pay. Everybody would chip in with something. The money would be put into a proper pay envelope and the clerk would solemnly pretend to check his name off the list.

Each night Sammy would be at the station, exactly ten minutes before the express was due. He would lope along the platform to the refreshment room. The girls on duty all knew the drill.

'Hi ya, Sammy!'

'Train on time, Sammy?'

'Gonna check out the fruit cake, Sammy?'

Having carefully sampled the cake, Sammy would give his big wave of approval and take off to the end of the platform. Taking out his watch, he would stand peering down the long glinting rails.

Passengers coming through the forty bends before our town often wondered at the apparent inconsistencies in the train's behaviour.

On some trips the train would roar through the bends, while the passengers lurched from side to side. Yet on the next trip, they might be almost in sight of town and the train would stop and wait for no apparent reason. It might do this, even when the signals were green all the way.

The answer was really quite simple. The train into Warramboo was never late and it was never early.

As the '30 Class' loco grunted into the station a small figure on the end of the platform would be seen holding up a big railway watch in one hand. With the other hand he would be waving the train in.

To be exactly on time was to win Sammy's ecstatic approval. With an enormous wave Sammy would signal his approbation and jog along beside the engine.

As the panting, hissing monster came to a stop, the coal-streaked face of the driver would split into a grin. Half stepping down from the cab, he would lift the little fellow onto the footplate.

'I'll check her out for you Sammy ... Steam ... a hundred and sixty ... OK? Water ... half a glass... OK? Air ... hundred pound ... right?'

Then carefully shepherding Sammy, the driver would open the fire door. Sammy would blink into the white incandescence with absorbed fascination. 'Nice bright fire, Sammy. No green fire into Warramboo.'

The ritual over and the door closed, Sammy would be lifted back to the platform. There he would stand, watching for the green light to wave from the guard's van. On the first swing of the lantern, his arm

'On some trips the train would roar through the bends, while the passengers lurched from side to side.' NSW SA

would sweep around and he would shout, 'OK George. Take her out!'

All drivers were George to Sammy.

There came one particular Sunday in winter. It was as cold as only Warramboo platform could be. Night had closed in and the rain had driven most of the waiting passengers into the refreshment room.

As the express crept in, it could be noticed that Old Angus, the permanent night porter, was behaving strangely. Instead of being at his proper post, he was standing outside the exit, squinting anxiously down the muddy road. As the train came to a halt, he shrugged and returned to his allotted position.

Old Angus was obviously disturbed; his usual pleasant courtesies were missing as he collected the tickets in moody silence.

At first he was hardly aware of the pressure on his back. Only when he felt a dragging pull on his coat did he bother to turn around.

The peaked little face was waxen under its incongruous railway cap. Sweat was pouring into the glassy unfocussed eyes.

'Oh you poor little devil.'

Bending quickly Old Angus scooped the frail form into his arms. He heard the raucous breathing and felt the heaving chest through the saturated coat.

Sammy died the next day with double pneumonia.

Believing that the express couldn't leave without him, he had dressed himself and somehow managed to get to the station.

The town put on one of the biggest funerals ever. Nearly all the railway people were there. Even the District Loco Engineer turned up.

Of course the old '30 Class' engines have been gone for years now. They have long been replaced by the big red diesels.

I went back to the old town a few weeks ago.

I smiled when the passengers lurched and complained as we hurtled through the forty bends.

As we finally passed through the ticket barrier, I remarked to the young man on the gate, 'Train's right on schedule, son.'

He looked at my pass; he obviously knew who I was.

'This is Warramboo Super ... you know ... into Warramboo the train is never late and it's never early.'

I nodded gently and glanced back at the swinging green lamp.

'OK Sammy,' I murmured. 'Take her out.'

# THE PUB WITH NO TRAIN

*by Russell Hannah & Jim Haynes*

'Where have you been, Henry? You're late again. I hope you've got a note from your mum.'

Leo the Lover was having his usual little dig at Henry the Hun, who, unlike Leo, was occasionally late arriving at the club for the afternoon drinking session.

'You're not going to use that weak excuse about the train being late again, are you?'

'I've been down to the Bloodhouse,' said Henry, and he took a good-sized swig from his first regulation schooner.

Now, the Bloodhouse is the local pub. It's called the Bloodhouse because of all the fights that take place there. It's an establishment mostly frequented by callow youths, bikies, layabouts, rogues and local ne'er-do-wells. There's a constant stream of loud music pumped through the bar. Rock bands perform there every second night and it is no place for a person who likes a quiet beer and a philosophical chat. Leo the Lover avoids it at all times.

Leo was, therefore, quite surprised to hear where Henry had been. He was curious as to why he would want to go there.

'What on earth were you doing at the Bloodhouse, Henry? I thought you were a bit too old to go near that place.' Leo couldn't resist a shot at Henry. 'I don't even drive past there meself,' he said, 'in case I get involved in a blue.'

'I had to see Hardware Herb,' Henry replied. 'He's going to donate a carton of beer to the war widows' Mother's Day raffle.'

Henry the Hun's annual effort for charity is the war widows' raffle for Mother's Day. Henry organises and runs the whole thing each year.

'When a publican offers to shout you a beer you can't really say no, can you?' Henry observed. 'Especially when he's donating to a good cause.'

'That raffle's just your attempt at atonement for what the Germans did in both world wars,' Leo remarked. 'You only do it once a year to try to prove you're a decent bloke.'

Henry disdainfully ignored Leo. His family have been in Australia for four generations; his father fought in World War II and his grandfather wore an Aussie uniform in World War I.

'Well, I had to have one beer with him out of sheer politeness, didn't I? Not that politeness is something you'd know about, Leo,' Henry remarked, getting a bit of his own back on the insult register. He took another large swig from his beer.

'Also,' Henry continued, after a long swallow, 'I happen to have known Hardware Herb for many years. When I was working as a painter for the Public Works up at Bardalungra, he was the publican at the Bardalungra pub. He's a miserable sort of bastard, but he always gives a carton of beer for the raffle 'cos we go back a long way.'

'How on earth did a publican end up with a name like "Hardware Herb"?' I asked, thinking there might be a good yarn in the explanation. Henry seemed in the mood for a yarn and I thought I'd divert the conversation away from the raffle so Leo and Henry wouldn't spend all evening insulting each other and getting narky.

Henry gave me one of those looks that indicated a certain pity mixed with exasperation. 'It's pretty simple, really,' he said as if talking to a kid. 'Before he was a publican he ran a hardware store.'

'Oh,' I remarked lamely. There was obviously no wonderfully riveting story in that nickname.

'Not that he was very good at that either,' Henry continued without any prompting. 'He's too bloody cranky to be any good at serving people or selling anything. He was always a bloody dreadful publican, too.'

'Nothing's changed then?' I put in, just to keep the conversation going.

'Well, you can see the sort of pub he runs now, and the one in Bardalungra was no better,' said Henry. 'In fact, it burned down not long after I left there.'

'Oh, how did that happen?' I asked, sensing that there might be a good yarn on offer, after all.

'Well ...' Henry began, warming to his task. 'The pub was called the Railway Hotel because it faced the railway station. But, as very few people travelled by train by the time Hardware Herb bought it, he was doing it a bit tough. The railway staff had been cut right back, too, so he got very little custom from them.

'Then they built a new highway that bypassed the pub, so even fewer people stopped for a beer 'cos it meant turning off the road. Old Herb was always whingeing that he could make a good living out of the pub if only it was on the highway. But of course, when the pub was built, there was no highway, only a railway line.'

'There was always a pub near the railway line in the old days,' put in Backhoe Bill, who had joined the table.

'Well, this pub was one of those big, old, wooden, double-storey places with high ceilings and cast-iron lace round the balcony,' continued Henry. 'It even had a cement watering trough and tethering rail for horses out the front. It was a lovely old pub.'

'Wait till I get the drinks,' I said, 'then tell us about the fire.'

Once drinks were refreshed, Henry carried on.

'Like a lot of those old buildings, the pub was a bit of a fire hazard. At least Hardware Herb must have thought so, 'cos he had it insured against fire for quite a lot of money. It carried enough insurance for him to be able to afford to build a modern brick tavern when it did burn down, anyway.'

'Oh, it was like that, was it?' I remarked.

'Yes,' Henry replied, 'it was quite a fire and caused a fair bit of discussion around the town.'

'Was anyone hurt?' I asked.

'Well, that was the funny thing,' continued Henry. He was obviously enjoying spinning the yarn right out now. 'Nobody was hurt. The odd thing was that when the fire started late one Saturday night, all the regular boarders had gone away for the weekend,' Henry paused, 'and evidently they'd taken their belongings with them.

'The other strange thing was that Hardware Herb had taken the wrought iron off the balcony a few days before and sent it down to the city to have it cleaned and painted. Apparently it was quite valuable.'

'Didn't anyone suspect something fishy?' I asked.

'Well, naturally the local sergeant came out to do a report. He had to determine where the fire started and what had caused it. Of course, he had to make a list of what had been destroyed for the insurance company. He asked Herb all the usual questions.'

'I suppose the sergeant had the usual small town relationship with the publican, too, so he wouldn't make it too difficult,' put in Leo.

'Yeah, the sergeant was a local bloke and had on a few occasions sampled Herb's limited hospitality,' Henry replied. 'But the funniest thing was when he decided to interview Herb's missus, just to make it look like he did a decent investigation.'

Henry paused to sip his beer. He seemed to be waiting for encouragement. He was enjoying himself now.

'Why was that funny?' I asked – because it appeared someone had to.

'Well,' Henry continued, lowering his glass, 'apparently when the sergeant asked Herb's missus, "Where were you when the fire started, Mrs Stevens?", she looked very uncomfortable, hesitated, and just looked at Herb.

'"It's all right, dear," Herb says to her, "just tell the sergeant where you were."'

Henry was enjoying himself so much he started to laugh at his own yarn.

'Would you like to let us in on the joke?' Leo asked him sarcastically. 'What did she bloody say?'

'Well, there's the sergeant with his notebook and pencil poised,' Henry chuckled, 'and she pipes up and says, "I was in the outdoor toilet where you told me to be, love."'

We all laughed then, enjoying a good yarn well told, and Backhoe asked, 'What happened?'

'As I said, the sergeant was a local bloke,' Henry replied. 'When the official inquiry was held, the cause of the fire was found to be "an electrical fault in the kitchen".'

'Sounds like the verdict should have been "accidental arson",' said Leo the Lover, who knows a thing or two about criminality. 'Happened a lot in the old days.'

'So, Hardware Herb got the insurance money and built a new pub, eh?' said Backhoe Bill.

'He certainly did. In fact he built a brand new single-storey brick and tile pub on the highway and business picked up straightaway. Another funny thing was that he somehow managed to save a lot of the old railway memorabilia and photographs from the old pub. He used 'em as decorations in the new pub.'

'Did he call it "the Railway Hotel", like the old one?' enquired Leo.

'No! He called it "Hardware Herb's Happy Accident Tavern".'

'Come off it, Henry,' said Leo with a chuckle. 'We both know he hasn't got that much initiative, let alone a sense of humour.'

'You're right,' grinned Henry the Hun. 'In fact what he called his new pub was "the Eldorado Tavern", perhaps because he reckoned it would turn into a gold mine. I guess he must have done well enough to sell it and buy the Bloodhouse, anyway.'

'Every bush town worth its salt had one pub known as the Bloodhouse,' said Leo, seizing the opportunity to start a yarn of his own. 'There was always one at the top end of town where the cockies, estate agents and commercial travellers used to drink. That pub was usually called "the Tattersalls", or "the Commercial", or "the Royal". At the other end of town there'd be the rough pub or "the Bloodhouse".

It was mostly the one near the railway station and it was always called "the Railway Hotel".'

'Sometimes there was one called "the Terminus", too,' added Backhoe Bill. Backhoe was a bit of a lateral thinker and often came up with these pieces of information.

'A lot of towns still have a Railway Hotel, though there hasn't been a train for years,' said Henry. 'Most towns have lost their rail service now, since they closed all the lines.'

'That's true,' said Leo, 'but there's one town that's got a Railway Hotel and it's never had a railway line through it, let alone a station.'

'You've always gotta go one better, haven't you?' said Henry.

'Well, it's true,' Leo replied smugly, 'and the reason that I know about it is that I had a beer and a feed there recently, and a great little pub it is too.'

'Hang on,' said Backhoe Bill, 'did you say this town *never* had a railway, but has a Railway Hotel?'

'Yeah, it's fair dinkum,' Leo replied. 'The place is called Wolumla. I ran across it when I was down the coast fishing a couple of years ago. I was driving between Bega and Merimbula and there it was, out in the middle of nowhere – the Railway Hotel, Wolumla.

'There's not a railway line to be seen. There never was a line at Wolumla or anywhere else on the South Coast for that matter. The nearest railway lines stopped a couple of hundred kilometres to the north at Bombaderry, and a hundred kilometres up the range at Bombala.'

'Well, there's gotta be a story in that,' I said. 'Did you stop to investigate?'

'Course I did,' said Leo the Lover. 'I went into the pub and had a beer and a spot of lunch.'

'Any excuse to stop and have a beer,' muttered Henry the Hun.

'I never need an excuse for a beer,' Leo shot back, 'but this was more like historical research, really.'

'Yeah, right,' said Henry.

'The publican seemed a decent sort of bloke,' Leo continued, 'and he told me the story. It seems that back in the late 1800s, when old Henry

Parkes was premier, he came down the coast campaigning. In those days you didn't promise tax cuts or border security to get votes. What you promised were public buildings and railways.'

'You couldn't bribe the voters by getting them drunk either,' Backhoe chimed in, 'because they used to shut the pubs on election day.'

Leo paused and regarded Backhoe expectantly, but no more information was forthcoming.

'Thanks for that piece of useless historical trivia,' said Leo over-politely. 'If you've no more grand political history to impart, I'll continue.'

'Okay,' said Backhoe Bill, 'I just thought you might like to know.'

'Well, it might come in handy one day, Backhoe,' I added, just to be part of the conversation.

'Anyway,' Leo continued, 'old Henry promised a lunatic asylum and a railway to Eden. The line was to come down the mountain from

The publican of the Railway Junction Hotel, Wolumla, still waiting for the train after more than a hundred years. RH

Railway Junction Hotel, Wolumla, soon after it was built. RH

Bombala, and Wolumla was to be the junction where the line would shoot off north to Bega.

'So, some enterprising developer decided to beat the crowd, get in first and build a Railway Hotel. The only problem was that the line was never built. So, right there at Wolumla, is the only Railway Hotel ever built without a railway. It's a good pub though.'

'How about the lunatic asylum?' asked Backhoe. 'Did they ever build that?'

'I don't think they did,' answered Leo. 'Maybe there weren't enough mad characters down there to warrant one.'

'Probably because most of the lunatics live around here,' said Henry the Hun draining his glass. 'And that happens to remind me — it's your shout, Leo.'

# TRAVELLIN'

*by Henry Lawson*

We were going at Christmas-time in a special holiday train over the Blue Mountains some twenty-seven years ago, and a robust voice was singing:

> *Hand the snow was lightly fallin'*
> *Hon 'er shoulders all the while.*

The singer was a slight, rather undersized bushman of the Nearer West, as it was then, of the better class, who leaned back luxuriously in his seat in the second-class carriage and enjoyed his singing. Luxuriously, I say, because it seemed to be a relief from the everlasting saddle-way of travelling.

He enjoyed his singing, I said, and so did I, a young workman sitting opposite him, who was going 'up the mountains', that had neither novelty, rest nor holiday in him; for he had a job there before, and was going up to another.

But we were happy travelling in those days, second-class or first; and the further some of us were going together the happier we were. Ways were never long and weary, nor dull and hot and dreary; and no one bothered about his watch or timetables, or asked how far it was to any station or what time we'd get there. The whisky flasks went round and the bottled ale went round; and very soon Christian names like Bill and Jim and Jack went round; and blokes and coves and fellers and chaps were given nicknames that lasted them to the journey's end and sometimes beyond it, amongst men who'd never seen each other in their lives before and might never meet again; and the brotherly joke went round at each other's expense, and there was all the best of good-fellowship, and we all were mates.

We never bothered about 'refreshments' on those journeys. We were too healthy and happy to eat – merely 'scoffed' a sandwich or two occasionally or tore at the leg or wing of a cold fowl. And that only out of politeness to the giver, perhaps some lovable and provident elderly party of the jovial, well-to-do digger persuasion. The sight of stout, black-coated persons of full habit of life, seriously, earnestly and even nervously anxious at their soup, with napkins up to their fat, white throats in the refreshment-rooms, always filled me with a strange sort of pity. The others regarded them (or didn't regard them) with utter indifference or as beneath contempt, or above it, if you like.

A peep into first-class carriages, when we got out to stretch our legs, mostly revealed stout, red-faced squatters of the old school who lived on their runs and had their womenfolk in reserved carriages away from them; and jolly, good-natured, healthy and honest-looking commercial travellers telling their yarns and cracking their jokes whereof the humour redeemed the smut. And young honeymoon couples evidently in a bad way.

In the next compartment there was a merry party of all sorts – young fellows from the city, but mostly in what are called the 'humbler walks of life'. But they weren't humble; they were too carefree to be humble, or anything else except happy. They had a keg of beer with a wooden tap, and it had a place on the seat no matter which one of them had to stand or squat on the floor. They took great care of that keg of beer, and their humourist (there was always one in those days) rested his arm and head lovingly on top of 'Bobby' and dozed between taps.

Now and again they'd hand a billy out through the windows into the next compartment for'ard of theirs, where a section of the party were; and then they'd hand a smaller billy past, per favour of us, into the next compartment aft of ours, where one or two stray members of their party were; and, anon, they'd hand the larger billy in to *us*. And so on, after what a French friend of mine used to call 'ze propaire interval'.

They got off at a thirty-minutes refreshment station, and the last we saw of them they were grouped behind the joker of the party, who was standing on Bobby selling the train, from engine to brake-van, with its contents, not forgetting the honeymoon couples; and the last we heard of them they were giving us three ringing cheers from the platform.

> *And the dust was lightly falling*
> *On her shoulders all the while.*
> *And the sods are lightly lying*
> *On her coffin all the while.*

Ah, well! Some of those merry, careless boys of '88 and '89 may be some of the hard, silent, sullen, suspicious elderly travellers I see now. I noticed the change in travelling before the war – long before. Coming down from Mudgee, second Easter before last, and over those same mountains, there were only silent, sullen, resentful men in our carriages, and a dusty, shabbily-creased, dispirited and uneasy shade of a jockey from the Mudgee racecourse. His faded and sickly-brown clothing had little three-cornered rents in it, as if he'd run through barbed wire fences from the course to the railway station. Probably he had good cause to run, as Mudgee (and all other) racing goes now. He seemed too furtive and unsubstantial even for it to be possible to take him up for anything. And there was the faded ghost of an old-time 'commercial' who clung to a Gladstone protected by a holland cover, evidently to help the illusion that it was still new. And a cranky Yorkshireman – and they *can* be cranky. And a disgruntled Kentish assisted-immigrant, returning from a job they'd got him in the Junee district, and telling the Yorkshireman how he'd knocked the boss off the plough and got his bundle and left. There was also something about 'these Australians'. I tried to promote conversation — it was a dead, blank failure. I asked a civil question and, failing to get an audible reply, I barked at them that I was deaf. It only elicited a sickly grin. The Australian seemed to have vanished and to be extinct. There *was* a tall, lank, sad, silent, elderly man, grey as a badger, who might have been a grinful Australian once; but he had grown too old and weary and careworn for the job, and had given it up in despair.

And now for another trip.

The Little Landlady is in a first-class for'ard with Nigger the cat. Charley the dog is in a compartment of his own in the brake-van aft. Charley belonged to the country — I don't know which part — and to a young soldier who took him down to the city and left him with 'friends' and went to the Front. Now he is going back to the country with a master who, I hope, will treat him as well as the first one did.

There are various little ways of doing our little bits. The Little Landlady, for instance, wanted to boil a bullock's heart and bring it with her, so that I might give Charley a slice or two at various stations.

Behind me a fortnight of nightmare, clearing up my own affairs and packing and carting furniture under the advice of a little woman who was worse when she tried to assist.

Farewells of, and to, belated friends; the last bell; the last kiss; the last clasp of hands; the whistle; and we are moving with all our loads of sins and sorrows and pains and cares, but still with a blessed relief and — thank God from whom all mercies fall!

The sleeping-car attendant is an old man — so old and faded that I shall not remember whether he had a moustache, side-whiskers or a short beard. The Old Guard. The Old Guard says they won't serve him at Moss Vale. So I have a beer, and produce another glass and put it on the bar and smile at the laughing girl there as if I know her. Probably I do. Anyway, I get a stiff nip for the Old Guard and slip aboard and put it under one of the seats; and presently — very presently — I see the Old Guard's shadow stoop to that seat, and then his shadow, glass in hand, reaches down the water carafe, dilutes sparingly and drinks. Shadow of a

Shadow, Old Guard! How many hands in the dead, dead past may not have lifted glasses to drink to you!

We move again. The Old Guard seems a trifle less shadowy and comes and sits by me thoughtfully till I go along and turn in. But not to sleep. Then the long roar – roar – roar-r-r, with the undercurrent of hum and buzz, with millions of z's in it, down into the Goulburn Valley.

Goulburn held no interest for me, except as regarded getting a beer; and I turned in again and tried to sleep, and failed. So I watched the embankments, grey fences and ghost bush race past in the half moonlight; and after that went into the smoke compartment and sat with several others who had murder, rape and embezzlement on their minds – or seemed to have. No one spoke. Wherefore, I turned in again, and this time I woke to sunlight.

Dry gullies; bleached and fire-blackened logs and stumps; blazing watercourses – just ashen clay-gutters in the scalded ground, where water seldom comes and never stays an hour; unutterable scrub. The posts of the very old fences are woolly grey and seem old, old as the dead trees and as forgotten. On clearer slopes for miles and miles the grass from the last rains is dry beyond dryness and tough beyond toughness. Everywhere the bleached pale gold of stubble. The land seems old, old and older to me. God! Ours is the oldest land on earth – it is old beyond anything.

I didn't wake in time for Cootamundra, and the Old Guard must have wanted his morning's nip, poor old chap! However, I'll fix him up all right at Junee. Whereat he confides to me concerning 'commercials'.

'If they want to give me a bob,' he says, 'let them *give* me a bob. And if they don't want to give me a bob, let them don't. But they always begin about here to find fault as an excuse for not givin' me anything.'

They look like that.

Wheat, wheat, wheat! Wheat on both sides as far as the eye can reach, and everywhere, if I'm not mistaken, the bronze of Farrer's wheat. The sun is up, but the homes are still at rest excepting where blue smoke from a kitchen chimney hints of a hearty breakfast. This is not sordid, slaving, cow-cocky country. It is Wheat!

'And so on to Yanco and Leeton.' NSW SA

Presently the 'commercials' begin to come out, stonily suspicious of everybody and of each other.

We change at Junee; and I spot dog Charley chained to a lamp-post on the platform and on the best of terms with the guards. He is specially demonstrative towards a young fellow in khaki who is going down by the next train. Perhaps he recognises the uniform. Something also seems to move this soldier-boy from the country, for he makes as if he'd almost take Charley up in his arms, big as he is.

On catching sight of me he sets up such a barking as I never heard from a dog before. Every dog has his day, but Charley must have had a very uncomfortable and anxious night of it. However, his troubles, which he never shows by any sign to anybody − except perhaps at times to me − will soon be all over now.

Wheat, wheat, wheat, wheat, wheat, wheat, wheat! Seas of it on both sides, and all to feed a great, ant-swarming, mostly useless city like

Sydney, or to be sent abroad to feed soldiers who are murdering each other for one man's hateful greed!

Narrandera, with hints of rocky outcrops, ivied red brick, picture-book little churches, and *real* homes and greenery; and so on to Yanco and Leeton, the irrigation area – to a new life in an old dead land that is being made to live again.

# SECOND CLASS WAIT HERE

*by Henry Lawson*

On suburban railway stations, you may see them as you pass,
There are signboards on the platforms saying, 'Wait here second class'
And to me the whirr and thunder and the cluck of running gear
Seem to be forever saying, saying 'Second class wait here.'

And the second class were waiting, in the days of serf and prince,
And the second class are waiting, they've been waiting ever since.
There are gardens in the background, and the line is bare and drear,
Yet they wait beneath a signboard, sneering 'Second class wait here.'

I have waited oft in winter, in the mornings dark and damp,
When the asphalt platform glistened underneath the lonely lamp.
And the wind among the wires, and the poplars bleak and bare,
Seemed to be for ever snarling, snarling 'Second class wait there.'

Out beyond the further suburb, 'neath a chimney stack alone,
Lay the works of Grinder Brothers, with a platform of their own;
And I waited there and suffered, waited there for many a year,
Slaved beneath a phantom signboard, telling our class to wait here.

'On surburban railway stations …' DF

Ah! A man must feel revengeful for a boyhood such as mine.
God! I hate the very houses near the workshop by the line;
And the smell of railway stations, and the roar of running gear,
And the scornful-seeming signboards, saying 'Second class wait here.'

There's a train with Death for driver, which is ever going past,
And there are no class compartments, and we all must go at last
To the long white jasper platform with an Eden in the rear;
And there won't be any signboards, saying 'Second class wait here.'

# THE DAY THE COAL BLEW AWAY

*by Russell Hannah & Jim Haynes*

It was a chill August day, one of those days when people pull their coats tightly around them and lean into the wind as they make their way home from whatever business may have led them outdoors. The kind of day when the westerly wind sweeps down the escarpment, whistling its contempt for mankind and all his creations.

Mind you, the wind had not reached its peak that day. When it did, it was capable of removing roofs, uprooting trees and leaving caravans lying on their sides like stranded whales.

Nevertheless, it was not a day to be outside. It was a day for feeling cosy, staying in and maybe reading a book, thumbing your nose at the noise outside and feeling safe. But, for my sins, I had to venture out to attend the opening of the Black Diamond Centre, an old miner's cottage recently restored by community volunteers and turned into a museum for the coal industry in the Illawarra district.

The local council, the coal unions and the government had thrown in a handful of money, and all the local notables were gathering to make speeches and have their photographs taken for both publicity and posterity. The minister for Heritage and Culture had arrived from the city and, accompanied by her minders, was the centre of attention for the mayor, the council's general manager and the local media. A sprinkling of the public attended, although their numbers had obviously been kept down by the weather. Of course the volunteers who had worked to bring the restoration into being were all there.

I was there because some years before, in a fit of misguided enthusiasm, I had stood for a seat on the local council and, to the surprise of many including myself, had been elected. In the short time I'd been on council I'd developed a healthy cynicism for the local government process. I'd also become heartily sick of settling disputes between neighbours over fences and barking dogs. I'd decided that there were better ways to spend my time and I'd determined not to stand again.

So, I'd been invited to the opening of the Black Diamond Centre as a councillor, but I would have been there anyway. It seems to me that too much of our history goes unrecorded, particularly that which involves ordinary people, often doing extraordinary things.

The speeches were made and the mayor and the minister duly had their photographs taken and received a smattering of polite applause. Then the refreshments were brought out – the usual tea, coffee, orange juice, wine, biscuits, cheese, sandwiches, cakes and savouries – a small reward to those who had braved the weather and the speeches to be part of the historic occasion.

I knew that my fellow local councillors would want to talk about the coming elections, in which I had little interest. So, to avoid getting drawn into this conversation, I grabbed my wine and cheese and headed to the back of the room, where there were at least a few interesting historical photographs to hold my attention.

It was then that I noticed an old fellow sitting quietly alone. He had a walking stick by his side and he seemed a little out of place among the dignitaries and middle-aged volunteers. I judged him to be well into his eighties, maybe even past ninety. His eyes were rheumy and his face was lined but firm. As I got closer I noticed the large arthritic hands that seemed to indicate a life spent in hard toil. His suit was an old navy-blue double-breasted and he wore a waistcoat over his white open-necked shirt. The suit pants had large cuffs and were held up by braces. He appeared to have stepped out of one of the many historical photos that adorned the walls.

I sat down and introduced myself. He just nodded and shook my hand. I had the feeling that he knew who I was, or at least knew I was a councillor. His hand was gnarled but the grip was firm. I realised later that he didn't tell me his name.

'Not much of a day to be out,' I said conversationally.

'I've seen a lot worse,' he said dryly.

'Lived around here long?' I asked, and immediately realised what a stupid question it was.

I knew he thought the same when he regarded me quizzically for a few moments before replying, 'All my life.'

I tried to make up some lost ground: 'I reckon you would have been a miner too.'

'Worked the old Excelsior Mine at Bulli most of my life,' he said, 'and my father worked there before me. So did three of my brothers. All dead now though.'

I worked the subject back to the museum. 'It's good to see this place open to preserve the old mining history, isn't it?' I asked.

'Well, yes it is,' he replied, 'but there's things that happened that you won't see hanging on the walls around here.'

'Yes,' I agreed, 'blokes like you probably carry more history in your heads than you can fit in a place like this.'

'Well, there's things that I know happened because I was there, that's true,' he said, and for the first time in the conversation a little fire seemed to burn in his eyes. 'I remember the strike back in 1938 — there's not much about that here.'

'I've heard it was tough going in the mines in those days,' I offered. 'That would have been just at the end of the Depression.'

'Everyone reckoned it was the end of the Depression but it wasn't for us miners,' he stated emphatically. 'It wasn't until the war started that the Depression was over. Until then the bosses had the upper hand and they'd screw you to make a few extra bob in profits to buy their new cars and houses.'

'I've heard about the Bulli miners' reputation for never taking a backward step in any fight with the bosses,' I said.

He looked at me thoughtfully. 'Most blokes didn't want to strike and struggle,' he said. 'They were just glad to get a wage. The memory of those awful Depression years was still too fresh in their memories, you see.

'But what you say is right – us miners at Bulli rarely took a backward step. We had a pretty good history of taking action to defend ourselves. Even in the great strike of 1886, when the government tried to break us by letting the criminals out of Darlinghurst Gaol if they'd come down and work in the Bulli mines.'

'Is that right?' I asked. 'I never knew that.'

'Yes, they did release them too, but the miners' wives sat in front of the train that brought them up from the jetty and stopped it. The train drivers weren't going to run over women and children.'

'The Mahatma Ghandi technique,' I said, airing my knowledge. 'Sit in front of the trains and dare them to run over you.'

'I reckon Mahatma Ghandi probably learnt that off the Bulli miners' wives,' he countered. 'It was years before he started non-violent confrontation in India. The wives held their babies up for the crims to see and asked them not to take the food out of their kids' mouths. Some of them had the decency to turn around and go right back to gaol, too, but there were still enough of them to eventually break the strike.

'Funny thing,' he said reflectively, 'the following year the pit blew up and eighty-one miners were killed. Nobody knows how many were strikebreakers from the gaol, but there were a lot of good men killed that day too. They've got a bit about that recorded here, not the full story though.'

'There's a monument to all those killed down in the churchyard, too,' I added. 'But what about the 1938 strike? Were you involved in that one?'

'Yes, the company tried to cut our pay by threepence a ton,' he explained. 'You see, we were all contract hewers of coal in those days. We used to get paid two shillings and nine pence a ton, and we'd generally pull out ten tons per day. Our motto was "Not a minute off the day, not a penny off the pay." Of course, when they tried to cut our pay, then the strike started.'

'I remember hearing about the bloke that led that strike,' I said. 'They used to talk about him a lot, but his name escapes me.'

'That'd probably be Fair-go McDonald.' His response was slow and measured.

'That's right, I remember now – I knew he had a nickname.'

'His real name was Arthur,' he chuckled.

'Do you know how he got the name "Fair-go"?'

'Well, I suppose it was because he always reckoned everyone deserved a fair go at meetings. If anyone was shouted down he'd say, "Give him a fair go, boys." And they reckoned he always finished his speeches with "All we want is a fair go."'

'What happened back in 1938?' I asked.

'Well, the company was holding out because they were happy to have us off the payroll. There was a fair bit of coal stockpiled and the market hadn't been real strong before the strike started. The thing they didn't like was being stood up to. The bosses thought miners had to do as they were told and work to the conditions that were laid down. They'd do anything they could to make the union weaker.'

'Not much they could do about it, though,' I remarked, 'if you were on strike and holding the line.'

'Not so,' he said, looking up at me. 'We got word that they were sending scabs from the city to load a train with coal to go up to the powerhouse at Bunnerong. Of course, as soon as we heard that, we called a meeting of the lodge.

'Some of the men wanted to take on the scabs and others didn't want to do anything at all. We knew there'd be a heavy police escort and we'd probably get our heads beaten and maybe get arrested. One thing all agreed on, though, was that we couldn't let them get away with it.'

He paused and surprised me with a laugh. 'Then we had this great idea, which was put to the men and carried unanimously.'

'A great idea?'

'Yes,' he went on. 'And when the scabs arrived there was no violence at all, except for some name-calling. Of course, they had a battalion of policemen surrounding them.'

'Ah well, I suppose coppers have a job to do as well.'

'You're right,' he agreed, 'and they have to do some distasteful things at times in the police force.'

'You still haven't told me what this great idea was,' I said. 'I'm curious.'

'I'm getting to that,' he said patiently. 'When the train was loaded they took the strikebreakers away to wherever scabs go at night. I can still see them marching off under escort.'

'Your memory's pretty good for all this,' I remarked, 'considering it was such a long time ago.'

'Easy to remember it today, because it was a day like this – a howling gale. It was a day you just wanted to stay huddled round the fire, but we had serious work to do.'

Bulli coal loaded for Bunnerong. WCL

'How could Fair-go stop the train once it was loaded and set off?' I asked.

'He didn't have to,' the old fellow replied. 'The train left the marshalling yards at Thirroul and it was already dark when it stopped at the Coalcliff Tunnel signals. It's a single line through the tunnel and coal trains don't have high priority. The train waited there about fifteen minutes and if it hadn't been dark, someone might have seen twenty or thirty figures climbing into the coal trucks with their faces blackened.

'The wind seemed to get stronger as the train moved slowly towards Waterfall. When it stopped to get the signal to come through Waterfall, twenty or thirty men with shovels climbed out of the coal trucks.'

We both laughed.

'Nobody saw a thing,' he grinned. 'It was dark and not the sort of night anybody wanted to be out and about.'

'Were the miners doing what I think they were doing?' I asked with a laugh.

'Well, put it this way,' he said, 'an inspector checked the load at Tempe a few miles down the track, and there was no coal at all in any of the trucks.'

We shared another laugh.

'The guard, driver and fireman were all questioned at length, but strangely nobody could shed any light on what had happened to the missing coal. They say the company bosses were furious.'

'I bet there was hell to pay.'

'Too right,' he said. 'The police were called in to investigate. Of course, every miner on the coast knew what had happened and so did the police but they couldn't prove a thing, and maybe they didn't want to anyway.'

'I bet old Fair-go had a good laugh about it all.'

He paused and grinned. 'Yes, he did, especially when the police came down to interview him.'

'Do you know what he told them?' I asked.

'I know exactly what he told them.' His eyes were now positively sparkling. 'He told them the same thing everybody else told them.

Empty coal train at Tempe Station. DF

"It must have been the wind," he said. "It was blowing a gale that night. I suppose the coal just blew away.""

'Well, it's an ill wind that doesn't blow somebody some good,' I commented.

'Too right, and I'll tell you another thing,' he went on, 'the miners who lived close to the track had another reason to be pleased about the powerful wind that night. You see, nobody had to buy coal for their fires for months. They'd just walk along the side of the line between Coalcliff and Waterfall and they could get all the fuel they needed.'

'What a great story. I bet miners still talk about how Fair-go McDonald made the coal blow away.'

'I don't know about that,' he said slowly. 'It was a long time ago and I think it's pretty much forgotten. Nothing here in this museum about it.'

'Well, it's a story that deserves to be right here in this museum,' I told him. 'Are any of the men still alive?'

'Only me, and I'm ninety-one.'

It was as if the mention of his age brought him back to the present. He sighed and blinked his old eyes. I straightened my back in my chair and suddenly realised that the crowd had thinned out and the dignitaries had all left.

I was about to say my goodbyes and thank him for the story when I felt a presence and turned to see a neat grey-haired woman standing patiently behind me.

'Come on, Dad,' she said to the old man, 'it's time I got you home. You've had a pretty big day and I think there's a bit of a lull in the wind outside.'

'You're right,' he agreed, 'I reckon I've had a pretty fair go ... Where's my stick?'

It was then that I realised who I'd been talking to.

'It's here, Mr McDonald,' I said, passing him the stick. 'And it's been a real pleasure talking to you.'

# BREAKFAST ON THE BANJO

*by Russell Hannah & Jim Haynes*

### THE BANJO

'Banjo' was a common term for a coal shovel used in both coal mining and railways. The name derives from the shape, which facilitated faster unloading of the shovel when the coal had to be thrown a distance. Shovels were classified by size — a number 5 banjo, etc. These shovels made perfect hotplates.

'I read,' said Henry the Hun, 'where all new diesel locos are going to have microwave ovens installed in their cabins.'

We were having our usual daily drink at the club and conversation was a little slow.

'Gee, all mod cons these day, eh?' said Backhoe Bill. 'I never had a microwave on me backhoe. Workers get spoiled these days.'

'I reckon it's a plot,' Leo the Lover chimed in, 'so they'll never have to stop for a crib or lunch break. It's this new drive for increased productivity. They've been pushing for this ever since they privatised all the freight lines.'

Leo is not over-fond of increasing productivity, particularly his own. Mind you, he wouldn't be against Cranky Cec the barman fitting a little more beer into his glass. That would enable him to drink a bit more in the two-hour 'session' he has every day at the club.

'Anyway,' continued Leo, who is not only an old railwayman himself but also the son of an engine driver, 'it's nothing new. My father always cooked his own meals in the old steam days.'

'They didn't have microwave ovens when your old man was around,' said Henry the Hun dismissively. Henry likes to catch Leo out if he thinks he's telling 'porkies'.

'I didn't say they had microwaves,' Leo replied, 'but they did have cooking facilities, and I'll tell you a story that proves it, whether you say it's the truth or not.'

'Well,' said Henry, 'when you tell stories we never know if they're true or not.'

'Well, my old dad never told a lie, not very often anyway,' said Leo, 'and this happened when Dad and his fireman were working a "goods" up near Garah on the North West line. The night was terrible cold, as nights are on the Western Plains in winter and this old fellow, a bit down on his luck, asked if he could get a ride with them. There were still swaggies around then, though they'd given up jumping into billabongs, and trains were still their favourite form of transportation.

'Now, the night being so cold, my old dad felt a bit sorry for him. So, rather than let him ride back on one of the flat cars where he might catch pneumonia, he invited him into the cabin.

'Of course, having unauthorised people in the loco cabin was a breach of several regulations and could lead to all sorts of punishment, including the sack. But they were pretty certain that they wouldn't run into any inspectors – it was a Sunday night and a bit too cold for inspectors to be out and about.

'The old fellow was very happy to sit unobtrusively in a corner where he could get very warm. He was still there a few hours later when morning came on and the train was parked in a siding to wait for a "down goods" to pass, it being a single line.

'"Time for breakfast," says Dad, and the fireman gets the tucker out. "You'd better join us," he said to the old fellow. The swaggie was very thankful and said that it was very kind of them to share their sandwiches with him.

'"Sandwiches," laughed my dad, "no one eats *sandwiches* for breakfast in my cabin. It's always a good solid Australian feed: sausages, bacon and eggs, toast, and a spot of Worcestershire sauce for a bit of flavour."

'Well, the old swaggie was delighted. He was amazed to hear that he was about to get some real tucker. Swaggies often had to make do with a "swaggie's breakfast" – drink of water, a smoke and a pee. He was a bit puzzled, however, and asked Dad how he planned to cook this feast. He didn't see any cooking facilities in the cabin.

'The fireman just chuckled and produced his shovel, which, though well used, was as clean and shiny on the action side as the day it was new. The constant scraping of the coal on the surface of a fireman's shovel always kept it clean. "Instant hotplate!" said the fireman. "Breakfast on the banjo!"

'Dad cracked a few eggs onto the shovel, threw on a bit of bacon and a couple of sausages; then the fireman held the shovel in the firebox and before long the three men were tucking into a great breakfast.

'"Better than sandwiches or a swaggie's breakfast, eh?" said my dad, sipping his tea.

'"Bloody oath!" said the old swaggie. "Best breakfast I've had since the ones me old mum cooked before I left home thirty years ago!" He reckoned that travelling with my dad and his mate was much better than travelling with the "toffs" in first class, though he had no experience of travelling with a ticket.

'By now they were taking the train along at the usual pace that goods trains go and the old fellow settled back in the corner of the cabin out of everyone's way. Before long he fell asleep as the train chuffed along.

'When the train started to pile on speed a couple of hours later, the swaggie woke up. It seems my dad had to make up time to get into the next passing loop and let a passenger train through. It's important that passenger trains aren't late. If they're held up people are likely to complain, so Dad was in a bit of a hurry and he couldn't stop anywhere.

'When the old fellow woke up he started to squirm a bit. He had a funny look on his face and Dad twigged to the problem at once. "Are you okay?" he asked.

Ken Williams, general manager of Australian Railways Historical Society Research Centre NSW, holding a fireman's shovel. RH

'Well, the old bloke looked a bit apologetic, evidently. He told Dad there was a bit of urgency about him finding a place where he could answer a very severe call of nature. It was probably partly due to the first decent feed of rich tucker he'd had in ages. "Does this loco have a dunny?" he asked.

'"Of course we've got a dunny, mate," my dad says with a grin. "Pass him the dunny, Bill." At this the fireman stopped leaning on the banjo and passed it to the old bloke.

'"Go for your life," said Dad, "but try to make it quick. It's nearly time for crib and I want to cook a couple of pancakes."

'My dad had no idea how that swaggie managed to hang on till he left them when they parked in the passing loop. "He didn't even thank us for breakfast," Dad said.

'So, you see,' Leo concluded, 'what they're proposing is nothing new. I bet those breakfasts cooked in the firebox on a banjo were tastier than any heated-up crap out of a microwave.'

'It sounds to me like the fireman's shovel was the Swiss Army Knife of the steam days,' said Backhoe, who is noted for his insightful comments on many issues.

'Yeah,' said Henry slowly. 'I was going to have a barbecue for tea tonight, but I think I'll just get some Chinese takeaway from the club instead after that story.'

'Well, in that case you've got enough time for one more beer,' said Leo. 'You'd better get yourself over to the bar and shout ...'

# THE REMITTANCE MAN

by *Robert Louis Stevenson & Lloyd Osbourne*
*(adapted from* **The Wrecker***)*

### ROBERT LOUIS STEVENSON
### IN AUSTRALIA

Australia's railways may not have figured over-much in the world's greatest literature, but the Illawarra line made a considerable impression on two world-famous, albeit rather different, English authors – Robert Louis Stevenson and D.H. Lawrence.

Lawrence's stay has been well documented. His account of a trip from Sydney down to Thirroul by train appears elsewhere in this collection. The train trip described in Lawrence's novel is over the very same stretch of line the protagonist labours to build and repair in this next story. Both authors were obviously impressed by the spectacular scenery of the Illawarra escarpment and the way the railway clings to the mountainside.

Stevenson's account is much less well known. It seems that, on one of his visits to Sydney, Robert Louis Stevenson experienced the dramatic rail trip and later incorporated what he saw into the novel *The Wrecker*, which he wrote in collaboration with his stepson, Lloyd Osbourne. The dramatic scenery suited Stevenson's melodramatic prose, and the problems and accidents being experienced along that length of track were big news during his visits to Sydney. The turmoil and loss of life involved in building the line fitted perfectly into the story of the remittance man Norris Carthew.

The novel is an interesting insight into the phenomenon of the remittance man, a fellow banished to the colonies for some social or legal misdemeanour at home and kept away from the mother country, and thus prevented from bringing continued shame on the family, by the means of being funded from home with a monthly remittance. This was certainly not an uncommon practice in the late nineteenth century.

The social themes of shame and redemption underscore a strong story line involving Carthew's many and varied colonial adventures. The local colour of accidents and engineering challenges on the escarpment railway during the period of the great landslides of 1889–90 provided a perfect background for the tortured and troubled personal world of the protagonist.

Norris Carthew was born disenchanted, the world's promises awoke no echo in his bosom, and the world's activities and the world's distinctions seemed to him equally without a base in fact. Yet the lad's faults were no great matter; he was diffident, placable, passive, unambitious, and unenterprising; life did not much attract him; he watched it like a curious and dull exhibition, not much amused, and not tempted in the least to take a part.

He liked the open air; he liked comradeship, it mattered not with whom, his comrades were only a remedy for solitude. And he had a taste for painted art. Norris was perhaps the first of his race to hold the pencil. The taste was genuine, it grew and strengthened with his growth; and yet he suffered it to be suppressed with scarce a struggle.

Time came for him to go to Oxford, and he resisted faintly. He was stupid, he said; it was no good to put him through the mill; he wished to be a painter. The words fell on his father like a thunderbolt, and Norris made haste to give way. 'It didn't really matter, don't you know?' said he. 'And it seemed an awful shame to vex the old boy.'

To Oxford he went obediently, hopelessly; and at Oxford became the hero of a certain circle. He was active and adroit; when he was in the humour, he excelled in many sports; and his singular melancholy detachment gave him a place apart. He set a fashion in his clique. Envious undergraduates sought to parody his unaffected lack of zeal and fear. Among other things, this formula embraced the dons; and though he always meant to be civil, the effect on the college authorities was one of startling rudeness. His indifference cut like insolence; and in some outbreak of his constitutional levity he was 'sent down' in the middle of the second year.

The event was new in the annals of the Carthews, and his father was prepared to make the most of it. It had been long his practice to prophesy for his second son a career of ruin and disgrace. He coupled his son's name with the gallows and the hulks, and spoke of his small handful of college debts as though he must raise money on a mortgage to discharge them.

'Authors were obviously impressed by the spectacular scenery of the Illawarra escarpment and the way the railway clings to the mountainside.' RH

'I'll tell you what, Father,' said Norris at last, 'I don't think this is going to do. I think you had better let me take to painting. It's the only thing I take a spark of interest in. I shall never be steady as long as I'm at anything else.'

'When you stand here, sir, to the neck in disgrace,' said the father, 'I should have hoped you would have had more good taste than to repeat this levity.'

The hint was taken and Norris was inexorably launched upon a backward voyage. He was planted in the diplomatic service and told he must depend upon himself.

He did so till he was twenty-five; by which time he had spent his money, laid in a handsome choice of debts, and acquired a habit of gambling which left him wrecked and helpless. Old Carthew once more repurchased the honour of his name, this time at a fancy figure; and Norris was set afloat again on stern conditions.

An allowance of three hundred pounds in the year was to be paid to him quarterly by a lawyer in Sydney, New South Wales. He was not to write. Should he fail on any quarter day to be in Sydney, he was to be held for dead, and the allowance tacitly withdrawn. Should he return to Europe, an advertisement publicly disowning him was to appear in every paper of repute.

Norris pocketed the money and the reproaches, obeyed orders punctually; took ship and came to Sydney.

Eighteen days after he landed, his quarter's allowance was all gone and he found himself reduced, in a very elegant suit of summer tweeds, to herd and camp with the degraded outcasts of the city. In this strait, he had recourse to the lawyer who paid him his allowance.

'Try to remember that my time is valuable, Mr Carthew,' said the lawyer. 'It is quite unnecessary you should enlarge on the peculiar position in which you stand. Remittance men, as we call them here, are not so rare in my experience; and in such cases I act upon a system. I make you a present of a sovereign; here it is. Every day you choose to call, my clerk will advance you a shilling; on Saturday, since my office is closed on Sunday, he will advance you half a crown. My conditions are these: that you do not come to me, but to my clerk; that you do not come here the worse of liquor; and you go away the moment you are paid and have signed a receipt. I wish you a good-morning.'

'I have to thank you, I suppose,' said Carthew. 'My position is so wretched that I cannot even refuse this starvation allowance.'

'Starvation!' said the lawyer, smiling. 'No man will starve here on a shilling a day. I had on my hands another young gentleman, who remained continuously intoxicated for six years on the same allowance.' And he once more busied himself with his papers.

In the time that followed, the image of the smiling lawyer haunted Carthew's memory. 'That three minutes' talk was all the education I ever had worth talking of,' says he. 'It was all life in a nut-shell. Confound it! I thought, have I got to the point of envying that ancient fossil?'

Every morning for the next two or three weeks, the stroke of ten found Norris, unkempt and haggard, at the lawyer's door. The long day and longer night he spent in the Domain, now on a bench, now on the grass under a Norfolk Island pine, the companion of perhaps the lowest class on earth, the Larrikins of Sydney.

Many a long dull talk he held upon the benches or the grass; many a strange waif he came to know; many strange things he heard, and saw some that were abominable. It was to one of these last that he owed his deliverance from the Domain.

He sat one morning near the Macquarie Street entrance, hungry, for he had gone without breakfast, and wet, as he had already been for several days, when the cries of an animal in distress attracted his attention. Some fifty yards away a party of the chronically unemployed had got hold of a dog, which they were torturing in a manner not to be described.

The heart of Norris, which had grown indifferent to the cries of human anger or distress, woke at the appeal of the dumb creature. He ran amongst the Larrikins, scattered them, rescued the dog, and stood at bay. They were six in number, but for once the proverb was right, cruelty was coupled with cowardice, and the wretches cursed him and made off.

This act of prowess had not passed unwitnessed. On a bench nearby there was seated a diminutive, cheerful, redheaded creature by the name of Hemstead. He was the last man to have interfered himself, for his discretion more than equalled his valour; but he made haste to congratulate Carthew, and to warn him he might not always be so fortunate.

'They're a dyngerous lot of people about this park. My word! It doesn't do to ply with them!' he observed, in that *Austrylian* English.

'Why, I'm one of that lot myself,' returned Carthew.

Hemstead laughed and remarked that he knew a gentleman when he saw one.

'For all that, I am simply one of the unemployed,' said Carthew, seating himself beside his new acquaintance, as he had sat (since this experience began) beside so many dozen others.

'I'm out of a plyce myself,' said Hemstead.

'You beat me all the way and back,' says Carthew. 'My trouble is that I have never been in one.'

'I suppose you've no tryde?' asked Hemstead.

'I know how to spend money,' replied Carthew, 'and I really do know something of horses and something of the sea.'

'Well, what do you think of the ryleways, then?' asked Hemstead.

'What do *you* think of them, if you come to that?' asked Carthew.

'Oh, I don't think of them; I don't go in for manual labour,' said the little man proudly. 'But if a man don't mind that, he's pretty sure of a job there.'

'By George, you tell me where to go!' cried Carthew, rising.

The heavy rains continued, the country was already over-run with floods; the railway system daily required more hands, daily the superintendent advertised; but 'the unemployed' preferred the resources of charity or crime, and a navvy, even an amateur navvy, commanded money in the market.

The same night, after a tedious journey, and a change of trains to pass a landslip, Norris found himself in a muddy cutting behind South Clifton, attacking his first shift of manual labour.

For weeks the rain scarce relented. The whole front of the mountain slipped seaward from above, avalanches of clay, rock and uprooted forest spewed over the cliffs and fell upon the beach or in the breakers. Houses were carried bodily away and smashed like nuts; others were menaced and deserted, the door locked, the chimney cold, the dwellers fled elsewhere for safety.

Night and day the fire blazed in the encampment; night and day hot coffee was served to the overdriven toilers in the shift; night and day the engineer of the section made his round with words of encouragement, hearty and rough and well suited to his men. Night and day, too, the telegraph clicked with disastrous news and anxious inquiry.

Along the terraced line or rail, rare trains came creeping and signalling; and paused at the threatened corner, like living things conscious of peril. The commandant of the post would hastily review his labours, make (with a dry throat) the signal to advance; and the whole squad would line the way and look on in choking silence, or burst into brief cheer as the train cleared the point of danger and shot on, perhaps through the thin sunshine between squalls, perhaps with blinking lamps into the gathering, rainy twilight.

One such scene Carthew will remember till he dies. It blew great guns from the seaward; a huge surf bombarded, five hundred feet below him, the steep mountain's foot; close in was a vessel in distress, firing shots from a fowling-piece, if any help might come. So he saw and heard her the moment before the train appeared and paused, throwing up a Babylonian tower of smoke into the rain and oppressing men's hearts with the scream of her whistle.

The engineer was there himself; he paled as he made the signal; the engine came at a foot's pace; but the whole bulk of the mountain shook and seemed to nod seaward, and the watching navvies instinctively clutched at shrubs and trees: vain precautions, vain as the shots from the poor sailors. Once again fear was disappointed; the train passed unscathed; and Norris, drawing a long breath, remembered the labouring ship and glanced below. She was gone.

So the days and nights passed: Homeric labour in Homeric circumstances. Carthew was sick with sleeplessness and coffee; his hands, softened by the wet, were cut to ribbons; yet he enjoyed a peace of mind and health of body hitherto unknown. Plenty of open air, plenty of physical exertion, a continual instancy of toil, here was what had been hitherto lacking in that misdirected life, and the true cure of vital scepticism.

To get the train through there was the recurrent problem; no time remained to ask if it were necessary. Carthew, the idler, the spendthrift, the drifting dilettante, was soon remarked, praised and advanced. The engineer swore by him and pointed him out as an example. 'I've a new chum, up here,' Norris overheard him saying, 'a young swell. He's worth any two in the squad.' The words fell on the ears of the discarded son like music; and from that moment, he not only found an interest, he took a pride, in his plebeian tasks.

The press of work was still at its highest when quarter day approached. Norris was raised to a position of some trust; at his discretion, trains were stopped or forwarded at the dangerous cornice near Clifton; and he found in this responsibility both terror and delight. The thought of the seventy-five pounds that would soon await him at the lawyer's, and of his own obligation to be present every quarter day in Sydney, filled him for a little while with divided councils.

Then he made up his mind, walked in a slack moment to the inn at Clifton, ordered a sheet of paper and a bottle of beer, and wrote, explaining that he held a good appointment which he would lose if he came to Sydney and asking the lawyer to accept this letter as an evidence of his presence in the colony and retain the money till next quarter day.

The answer came in course of post, and was not merely favourable but cordial. 'Although what you propose is contrary to the terms of my instructions,' it ran, 'I willingly accept the responsibility of granting your request. I should say that I am agreeably disappointed in your behaviour. My experience has not led me to found much expectations on gentlemen in your position.'

The rains abated, and the temporary labour was discharged; not Norris, to whom the engineer clung as to found money; not Norris, who found himself a ganger on the line in the regular staff of navvies. His camp was pitched in a grey wilderness of rock and forest, far from any house; as he sat with his mates about the evening fire, the trains passing on the track were their next and indeed their only neighbours, except the wild things of the wood. Lovely weather, light and monotonous employment, long hours of somewhat campfire talk.

There were also long sleepless nights, when he reviewed his foolish and fruitless career as he rose and walked in the moonlit forest. There was also an occasional paper of which he would read all the advertisements with as much relish as the text: such was the tenor of existence which soon began to weary and harass him. He lacked and regretted the fatigue, the furious hurry, the suspense, the fires, the midnight coffee, and the rude and mud-bespattered poetry of the first toilful weeks.

In the quietness of his new surroundings, a voice summoned him from his exorbital part of life, and about the middle of October he threw up his situation and bade farewell to the camp of tents and the shoulder of Bald Mountain.

Clad in his rough clothes, with a bundle on his shoulder and his accumulated wages in his pocket, he entered Sydney for the second time, and walked with pleasure and some bewilderment in the cheerful streets, like a man landed from a voyage.

The sight of the people led him on and at last he came to the Domain and strolled there. He remembered his shame and sufferings, and looked with poignant curiosity at his successors. Hemstead, not much shabbier and no less cheerful than before, he recognised and addressed like an old family friend.

'That was a good turn you did me,' said he. 'That railway was the making of me. I hope you've had luck yourself.'

'My word, no!' replied the little man. 'There's no positions goin' that a man like me would care to look at.' And he showed Norris his certificates and written characters, one from a grocer in Woolloomooloo, one from

'His camp was pitched in a grey wilderness of rock and forest, far from any house.' WCL

an ironmonger, and a third from a billiard saloon. 'Yes,' he said, 'I tried bein' a billiard marker. It's no account; these lyte hours are no use for a man's health. I won't be no man's slyve,' he added firmly.

On the principle that he who is too proud to be a slave is usually not too modest to become a pensioner, Carthew gave him half a sovereign, and departed.

# MEN OF STEEL

*by Grahame Watt*

*They served their time in the harshest clime,*
*Without credit, without fame,*
*Through rock and sand they tamed the land,*
*Those men who bore the name ... the fettlers.*

*The Navvies, the fettlers, the men who laid the track,*
*They opened up Australia and tamed the raw outback.*
*From Tasmania's freezing wilderness to Queensland's blazing sun,*
*From Sydney right across to Perth, they battled and they won.*

*They suffered all the elements, winters bitter cold,*
*The heat of outback summer ... adversities untold.*
*They came from many nations and mostly came to stay,*
*They helped to make Australia the place it is today.*

*With nothing but a survey line they swung their picks for years,*
*They fought their way through parts unknown, those Aussie Pioneers.*
*Blasting rocks and bridging creeks, the rails were laid along,*
*The spikes were hammered firmly, the fishplates bolted strong.*

*The fettlers are forgotten when historians maintain,*
*'What made our nation prosper was the steam and diesel train.'*
*Who was it made it possible? Who was it made it real?*
*The navvies and the fettlers — Australia's men of steel.*

'The Navvies, the fettlers, the men who laid the track ...' Top: NTL JB; Bottom: NTL FPPU

# STARGAZER JONES

*by Russell Hannah*

Port Kembla has always been a working-class town. It was always home to the mighty BHP steelworks, where over 20 000 workers earned their living. It used to be said that if the steelworks coughed, the Illawarra developed a cold.

In the 1940s whole suburbs grew up around the works. The area prospered, there was no unemployment and the men who worked there brought home a liveable wage. The '40s and '50s saw a great expansion in the region; the harbour was home to a fleet of iron-ore carriers and company trains brought coking coal down from the mines in the Illawarra escarpment.

Port Kembla Railway Station was also the terminus for the branch line from Wollongong. The railway not only took the steel products to Sydney, it also carried a human cargo of workers to and from the works and dropped workers off at Lysaghts and Cringilla.

A train trip was an integral part of people's lives back then; cars were a luxury. Working people all travelled by train or bus, not only to work but also when they went on excursions or picnics or visited Sydney, a couple of hours away. The trains were most often hauled by 32 Class locomotives, those old workhorses of the New South Wales rail system.

Even when it came to marriages and honeymoons, most people went by train. The favourite spot for working-class honeymoons was the Blue

Mountains. Grand old hotels, like the Hydro Majestic at Medlow Bath and the Carrington at Katoomba, sat beside railway stations. They were the favourite honeymoon destinations for the newlyweds of the Illawarra.

Most weddings were held on Saturdays, as they still are. After a short reception the bride and groom would change into their going-away gear and, accompanied by the guests, they would head off to the railway station.

And what a gala occasion it was at the station when several wedding parties arrived to catch the same train. Ribbons, confetti, cheering, chiacking and even a spot of drinking gave the normally sombre station a carnival atmosphere with lots of bonhomie and goodwill.

The most popular train for honeymooners was the 5.50 pm bound for Sydney, where the transfer was made to the Blue Mountains train. It wasn't long before locals christened this train 'the Honeymoon Express'. The best man used to pop up to see the driver before the train pulled out, slipping him a couple of shillings to make sure that the whistle was blown regularly until the train moved out of earshot, much to the delight of the guests and the feigned embarrassment of the newlyweds. Drivers with a sense of humour often used to play 'Cock a Doodle Doo' on their train whistles.

Now, one of the most famous drivers on the NSW Railways was a chap called Stargazer Jones. He was not known as Stargazer because of any great interest in astronomy, but because he had a certain vagueness and forgetfulness about him. He was often in receipt of 'blueys', or 'please explain' directives that led to official reprimands and fines, for running signals, exceeding speed limits and other such misdemeanours. Still, he was a good-hearted fellow, and though he was often the victim of practical jokes, he rarely held a grudge.

For some time in the early '50s the other member of Stargazer's crew was a fireman named Paul O'Brien. Paul was a competent amateur ventriloquist and entertainer. He had, in fact, appeared on the very popular *Amateur Hour* radio show hosted by Terry Dear, winning the first prize one night with an act that consisted of imitating bird and animal noises. There weren't many birds or animals Paul couldn't imitate and workmates often heard kookaburras laughing or horses neighing or even lions roaring in the shower block when Paul was in overnight railway barracks.

Paul also had a wicked sense of humour.

One Saturday night, Stargazer and Paul were working the Honeymoon Express. After several best men from the wedding parties had crossed Stargazer's palm with the appropriate silver coins to ensure the whistle was blown, he was approached by another well-dressed fellow carrying a sugar bag.

'Look,' said the man. 'In this bag is my wife's cat. I am not fond of cats but I can normally tolerate them, particularly if it keeps my wife happy.

'She loves this cat but I find it obnoxious, especially when I am eating my dinner as it has a disturbing habit of jumping on the table and trying to steal whatever I am eating. No matter how well fed the cat is, it persists in this behaviour. I can stand it no longer and I have decided to rid myself of this cat once and for all.'

Though Stargazer Jones and his fireman listened intently, they wondered what all this had to do with them.

'I cannot,' the man continued, 'bring myself to drown the cat or do anything else that may lead to its death. Firstly, I am a bit soft-hearted and, secondly, I would have to lie to my wife. Unfortunately my wife always knows when I am lying and my life would be extremely miserable if she knew I had killed her cat. I just want it to disappear, and this is where you can help.'

'What can we do?' asked the bemused Stargazer Jones.

'What I would like you to do,' the man replied, 'is to release the cat from the bag as you are passing through the national park. That way the cat can have a good life roaming free and I can truthfully say to my wife that I have not harmed the cat in any way.

'Of course, I would like you to take this five shillings as a token of my appreciation for all your help.'

Well, Stargazer always had a soft spot for animals, especially when there was five bob involved. He thought this was a humane way of solving the problem and took the bag with the cat in it and placed it in the cabin. (This was, of course, in a less environmentally friendly time, when many people thought it was quite all right to let cats loose in national parks, much kinder in fact than drowning them.)

Stargazer had quite warmed to the Catman and they were passing the time of day chatting about cats and wives and life in general before the train departed. Meanwhile, Paul O'Brien, who had heard the entire conversation, moved the sugar bag to the other side of the cab, undid the string and released the cat on the other side of the train. In its place he stuffed a large lump of coal into the bag.

Soon the time came for the train to depart and, to the usual accompaniment of whistles, singing, waving and shouting, the honeymooners were left to hold hands in the carriages and contemplate their future lives as the train puffed towards Sydney via Wollongong.

Up in the cabin all was normal until the train approached Lysaghts. At that point Paul used his twin talents of ventriloquism and animal noise imitation, and Stargazer believed he heard a plaintiff cry come from the bag. The immediate response from the fireman was to give the bag a thorough kick, upon which Stargazer heard an even louder wail.

Stargazer was shocked at what he thought was a wanton act of cruelty to a dumb animal and admonished his fireman. 'Leave that cat alone,' he said. 'Even if it is making a bit of noise, it's not hurting anyone; I'll let it out when we get through Helensburgh.'

Another mile or so up the track, however, the same thing happened again, and the normally easygoing Stargazer was starting to get a bit annoyed with his fireman's apparent cruelty.

'I said, leave that cat alone,' he repeated. 'It'll be gone when we get into the park.'

The final act of the charade occurred as the train was pulling into Wollongong Station. Stargazer again heard a piteous meowing, and this time Paul O'Brien shouted 'I hate bloody cats!', picked up the sugar bag and hurled it into the blazing firebox. As he did so there was one last terrible scream of pain and then the fireman slammed the firebox door shut.

Well, Stargazer was absolutely mortified by Paul's behaviour, so much so that he overshot Wollongong Station and consequently earned himself another bluey. After an initial burst of angry shouting at his fireman, he subsided into a sullen silence.

The Honeymoon Express leaves Port Kembla Station. wcl

Apart from the cruelty to the cat, Stargazer felt that he had betrayed the trust of the bloke at Port Kembla Station. After all, he had promised him that no harm would come to the cat and it would be released to live a free life in the Royal National Park.

Paul O'Brien managed to control himself and keep from laughing even though he had to put up with a stony silence from Stargazer all the way to Central Station. It was such a good story that it wasn't long before every driver and fireman in the depot knew about it.

Everyone decided it was such a good story, in fact, that there was no one who would tell Stargazer about the hoax. Instead they milked it for all it was worth. Men would sidle up to him and tell him stories about cat skins being found outside Chinese restaurants, and they'd wonder what roast cat would smell and taste like. Others talked incessantly about cats having nine lives and some wondered aloud if the Port Kembla cat had used up eight of his lives somewhere else.

All this only encouraged Stargazer to hold firm to his one act of retribution: he refused to talk to his fireman. All ensuing journeys were undertaken in deathly silence and any talk was confined to the absolute bare essentials needed to run the train.

It was nearly killing Paul O'Brien not to confess, and the silence at work wasn't very pleasant, but so many people were getting mileage out of the story that he managed to endure the silence until the joke finally ran its course. And soon enough, it did run its course.

Two weeks after the incident, Stargazer and Paul were again at the head of the Honeymoon Express, about to pull out of Port Kembla Station, when Stargazer spotted the Catman striding down towards the loco. It was too late for Stargazer to hide; he had been spotted and he could see that the fellow was not at all happy as he approached.

'You know I trusted you,' the cranky Catman exclaimed. 'In good faith I gave you five shillings to get rid of the cat. You promised to let him out at the national park.

'Instead, what happens? I call in at the Commercial for a couple of schooners to celebrate at last being able to eat my tea in peace, and when I get home, what do I find? The bloody cat sitting on the table waiting for me!'

Stargazer was so relieved that the cat hadn't met a fiery fate that he was struck dumb for a minute. In that time, while the Catman waited for a reply, Stargazer at last realised that he'd been had. Then he remembered Paul's win in the amateur hour and the penny dropped – and he started laughing in the poor bloke's face. He was lucky the bloke didn't clock him one.

Stargazer finally gathered his scattered wits and assured the man that he was laughing with *relief*. 'You mustn't have had the bag tied tight enough, mate,' he lied. 'The cat escaped near Coniston. I've been really worried about it …' He finally managed to placate the Catman by promising to give him his five bob back or take the cat on another trip.

And the story of Stargazer Jones and the cat has gone down in the annals of railway folklore – well, here it is still being told over fifty years after the event. Some old railwaymen even credit the story with being the origin of the expression 'Letting the cat out of the bag'.

# LAURA GOES TO SCHOOL

*by Henry Handel Richardson*
*(adapted from* **The Getting of Wisdom***)*

In the passage, Sarah was busy roping a battered tin box. With their own hands the little boys had been allowed to paste on this a big sheet of notepaper, which bore, in Mother's writing, the words:

*Miss Laura Tweedle Rambotham*
*The Ladies' College*
*Melbourne*

Mother herself was standing at the breakfast-table cutting sandwiches. 'Come and eat your breakfast, child,' she said.

Laura sat down and fell to with appetite, but also with a side-glance at the generous pile of bread and meat growing under Mother's hands.

'I shall never eat all that,' she said ungraciously; it galled her to be considered a greedy child with an insatiable stomach.

'I know better than you do what you'll eat,' said Mother. 'You'll be hungry enough by this evening I can tell you, not getting any dinner.'

Pin's face fell at this prospect. 'Oh, Mother, won't she really get any dinner?' she asked; and to her soft little heart going to school began to seem one of the blackest experiences life held.

'Why, she'll be in the train, stupid, 'ow can she?' said Sarah. 'Do you think trains give you dinners?'

'Oh, Mother, please cut ever such a lot!' begged Pin, sniffing valiantly.

Laura began to feel somewhat moved herself at this solicitude, and choked down a lump in her throat with a gulp of tea. But when Pin had gone with Sarah to pick some nectarines, Mother's face grew stern, and Laura's emotion passed.

'I feel more troubled about you than I can say, Laura. I don't know how you'll ever get on in life – you're so disobedient and self-willed. It would serve you very well right, I'm sure, if I didn't give you a penny of pocket money to take to school.'

Then Sarah's voice was heard calling, and the boys went out into the road to watch for the coach. Laura's dressing proved a lengthy business, and was accomplished amid bustle, and scolding, and little peace-making words from Pin; for in her hurry that morning Laura had forgotten to put on the clean linen Mother had laid beside the bed, and consequently had now to strip to the skin.

The boys announced the coming of the coach with shrill cries, and simultaneously the rumble of wheels was heard. Sarah came from the kitchen drying her hands, and Pin began to cry.

'Now, shut up, res'vor!' said Sarah roughly: her own eyes were moist. 'You don't see Miss Laura be such a silly-billy. Anyone 'ud think you was goin', not 'er.'

The ramshackle old vehicle, one of Cobb's Royal Mail Coaches, big-bodied, lumbering, scarlet, pulled by two stout horses, drew up before the door, and the driver climbed down from his seat.

'Now good day to you, ma'am, good day, miss' – this to Sarah who, picking up the box, handed it to him to be strapped on under the apron. 'Well, well, and so the little girl's a goin' to school, is she? My, but time flies! Well do I remember the day, ma'am, when I drove you all across for the first time. These children wasn't big enough then to git up and down be thimselves. Now I warrant you they can – just look at 'em, will you? But my! Ain't you ashamed of yourself' – he spoke to Pin – 'pipin' your eye like that? Why, you'll flood the road, if you don't hold on. – Yes, yes, ma'am, bless you, I'll look after her, and put her inter the train wid me own han's. Don't you be oneasy. The Lord he cares for the widder and the orphun, and if He don't, why Patrick O'Donnell does.'

This was O'Donnell's standing joke; he uttered it with a loud chuckle. While speaking he had let down the steps and helped the three children up – they were to ride with Laura to the outskirts of the township. The little boys giggled excitedly at his assertion that the horse would not be equal to the weight. Only Pin wept on, in undiminished grief.

'Now, Miss Laura.'

'Now, Laura, good-bye, darling. And do try and be good. And be sure you write once a week. And tell me everything. Whether you are happy – and if you get enough to eat – and if you have enough blankets on your bed. And remember always to change your boots if you get your feet wet. And don't lean out of the window in the train.'

For some time past Laura had had need of all her self-control, not to cry before the children. As the hour drew near it had grown harder and harder; while dressing, she had resorted to counting the number of times the profile of a Roman emperor appeared in the flowers on the wallpaper. Now the worst moment of all was come – the moment of good-bye. She did not look at Pin, but she heard her tireless, snuffly weeping, and set her own lips tight.

'Yes, Mother … no, Mother,' she answered shortly. 'I'll be all right. Good-bye.' She could not, however, restrain a kind of dry sob, which jumped up her throat.

When she was in the coach Sarah, whom she had forgotten, climbed up to kiss her; and there was some joking between O'Donnell and the servant while the steps were being folded and put away. Laura did not smile; her thin little face was very pale. Mother's heart went out to her in a pity, which she did not know how to express.

'Don't forget your sandwiches. And when you're alone, feel in the pocket of your ulster and you'll find something nice. Good-bye, darling.'

'Good-bye … good-bye.'

The driver had mounted to his seat, he unwound the reins, cried 'Get up!' to the two burly horses, and the vehicle was set in motion and trundled down the main street. Until it turned the corner by the Shire Gardens, Laura let her handkerchief fly from the window. Sarah waved hers; then wiped her eyes and lustily blew her nose. Mother only sighed.

'It was all she could do to keep up,' she said as much to herself as to Sarah. 'I do hope she'll be all right. She seems such a child to be sending off like this. Yet what else could I do? To a State School, I've always said it, my children shall never go – not if I have to beg the money to send them elsewhere.'

But she sighed again, in spite of the energy of her words, and stood gazing at the place where the coach had disappeared. She was still a comparatively young woman, and straight of body; but trouble, poverty and night watches had scored many lines on her forehead.

As long as the coach rolled down the main street Laura sat bolt upright at the window. In fancy she heard people telling one another that this was little Miss Rambotham going to school. She was particularly glad that just as they went past the Commercial Hotel, Miss Perrotet, the landlord's red-haired daughter, should put her fuzzy head out of the window; for Miss Perrotet had also been to boarding-school, and thought very highly of herself in consequence, though it had only been for a year, to finish. At the National Bank the manager's wife waved a friendly hand to the children, and at the Royal Mail Hotel, where they drew up for passengers or commissions, Mrs Paget, the stout landlady, came out, smoothing down her black satin apron.

'Well, I'm sure I wonder your ma likes sendin' you off so alone.'

The ride had comforted Pin a little; but when they had passed the chief stores and the flourmill, and were come to a part of the road where the houses were fewer, her tears broke out afresh. The very last house was left behind, the high machinery of the claims came into view, and the watery flats where Chinamen were forever rocking wash dirt in cradles; and O'Donnell dismounted and opened the door. He lifted the three out one by one, shaking his head in humorous dismay at

Pin, and as little Frank showed signs of beginning, too, by puckering up his face and doubling up his body, the kindly man tried to make them laugh by asking if he had the stomach-ache. Laura had one more glimpse of the children standing hand in hand – even in her trouble Pin did not forget her charges – then a sharp bend in the road hid them from her sight.

She was alone in the capacious body of the coach, alone, and the proud excitement of parting was over. The staunchly repressed tears welled up with a gush, and flinging herself down across the seat she cried bitterly. It was not a childishly irresponsible grief like Pin's: it was more passionate, and went deeper; and her overloaded feelings were soon relieved. But as she was not used to crying, she missed the moment at which she might have checked herself, and went on shedding tears after they had become a luxury.

No one else got in, and when they had passed the only two landmarks she knew – the leprous Chinaman's hut and the market garden of Ah Chow, who twice a week jaunted at a half-trot to the township with his hanging baskets, to supply people with vegetables – when they had passed these, Laura fell asleep. She wakened with a start to find that the coach had halted to apply the brakes, at the top of a precipitous hill that led down to the railway township. In a two-wheeled buggy this was an exciting descent; but the coach jammed on both its brakes, moved like a snail, and seemed hardly able to crawl.

At the foot of the hill the little town lay sluggish in the sun. Although it was close on midday, but few people were astir in the streets; for the place had long since ceased to be an important mining centre: the chief claims were worked out; and the coming of the railway had been powerless to give it the impetus to a new life. It was always like this in these streets of low, verandahed, redbrick houses, always dull and sleepy, and such animation as there was, was invariably to be found before the doors of the many public houses.

At one of these the coach stopped and unloaded its goods, for an interminable time. People came and looked in at the window at Laura, and she was beginning to feel alarmed lest O'Donnell, who had gone inside, had forgotten all about her having to catch the train, when out he came, wiping his lips.

'Now for the livin' luggage!' he said with a wink, and Laura drew back in confusion from the laughter of a group of larrikins round the door.

It was indeed high time at the station; no sooner was her box dislodged and her ticket taken than the train steamed in. O'Donnell recommended her to the guard's care; she shook hands with him and thanked him, and had just been locked into a carriage by herself when he came running down the platform again, holding in his hand, for everyone to see, the apple, which Laura believed she had safely hidden under the cushions of the coach. Red to the roots of her hair she had to receive it, before a number of heads put out to see what the matter was, and she was even forced to thank O'Donnell into the bargain. Then the guard came along once more, and told her he would let no one get in beside her: she need not be afraid.

'Yes. And will you please tell me when we come to Melbourne.'

Directly the train was clear of the station, she lowered a window and, taking aim at a telegraph post, threw the apple from her with all her might. Then she hung out of the window, as far out as she could, till her hat was nearly carried off. This was the first railway journey she had made by herself, and there was an intoxicating sense of freedom in being locked in, alone, within the narrow compass of the compartment. She was at liberty to do everything that had previously been forbidden her: she walked up and down the carriage, jumped from one seat to another, then lay flat on her back singing to herself, and watching the telegraph poles fly past the windows, and the wires mount and descend. – But now came a station and, though the train did not stop, she sat up, in order that people might see she was travelling alone.

She grew hungry and attacked her lunch, and it turned out that Mother had not provided too much after all. When she had finished, had brushed herself clean of crumbs and handled, till her finger-tips were sore, the pompous half-crown she had found in her pocket, she fell to thinking of them at home, and of what they would now be doing. It was between two and three o'clock: the sun would be full on the flagstones of the back verandah; inch by inch Pin and Leppie would be driven away to find a cooler spot for their afternoon game, while little Frank slept, and Sarah splashed the dinner-dishes in the brick-floored kitchen. Mother sat sewing, and she would still be sitting there, still sewing, when the shadow of the fir tree, which at noon was shrunken like a dwarf, had stretched to giant size, and the children had opened the front gate to play in the shade of the public footpath. – At the thought of these shadows, of all the familiar things she would not see again for months to come, Laura's eyelids began to smart.

They had flashed through several stations; now they stopped; and her mind was diverted by the noise and bustle. As the train swung into motion again, she fell into a pleasanter line of thought. She painted to herself, for the hundredth time, the new life towards which she was journeying, and, as always, in the brightest colours.

She had arrived at school, and in a spacious apartment, which was a kind of glorified Mother's drawing room, was being introduced to a bevy of girls. They clustered round, urgent to make the acquaintance of the newcomer, who gave her hand to each with an easy grace and an appropriate word. They were too well-bred to cast a glance at her clothes, which, however she might embellish them in fancy, Laura knew were not what they ought to be: her ulster was some years old, and so short that it did not cover the flounce of her dress, and this dress, and her hat with it, were Mother's taste, and consequently, Laura felt sure, nobody else's. But her new companions saw that she wore these clothes with an elegance that made up for their shortcomings; and she heard them whisper: 'Isn't she pretty? What black eyes! What lovely curls!' But she was not proud, and by her ladylike manners soon made them feel at home with her, even though they stood agape at her cleverness: none of *them* could claim to have absorbed the knowledge of a whole house.

With one of her admirers she had soon formed a friendship that was the wonder of all who saw it: in deep respect the others drew back, forming a kind of allée, down which, with linked arms, the two friends sauntered, blind to everything but themselves. – And having embarked thus upon her sea of dreams, Laura set sail and was speedily borne away.

'Next station you'll be there, little girl.'

She sprang up and looked about her, with vacant eyes. This had been the last stoppage, and the train was passing through the flats. In less than two minutes she had collected her belongings, tidied her hair and put on her gloves.

Some time afterwards they steamed in alongside a gravelled platform, among the stones of which a few grass-blades grew. This was Melbourne. At the nearer end of the platform stood two ladies, one stout and elderly in bonnet and mantle, with glasses mounted on a black stick, and short-sighted, peering eyes; the other stout and comely, too, but young, with a fat, laughing face and rosy cheeks. Laura descried them a long way off; and, as the carriage swept past them, they also saw her, eager and prominent at her window. Both stared at her, and the younger lady said something, and laughed. Laura instantly connected the remark, and the amusement it caused the speaker, with the showy red lining of her hat, at which she believed their eyes had been directed. She also realised, when it was too late, that her greeting had been childish, unnecessarily effusive; for the ladies had responded only by nods. Here were two thrusts to parry at once, and Laura's cheeks tingled. But she did not cease to smile, and she was still wearing this weak little smile, which did its best to seem easy and unconcerned, when she alighted from the train.

# THE END OF THE LINE

*by Russell Hannah & Jim Haynes*

'Where's Leo the Lover?' asked Henry the Hun.

Henry had just entered the club and found, to his surprise, that the space under the TV set, usually filled by Leo the Lover, was vacant.

It wasn't only a surprise to Henry. It was a shock to most of the other drinkers in the club. Even Cranky Cec, the barman, not usually a fan of Leo's, was a bit concerned and there was some discussion in the club as to where Leo the Lover could be. No one could recall a night when Leo was not ensconced under the TV set at his appointed time.

One of the more extreme suggestions was that he might have died. Others thought he might have merely been severely ill.

Henry the Hun bought himself a calming drink, returned to the table, and actually said a few kind words about Leo, just in case he really was dead. These kind words were cut short when a stranger entered the club and had the effrontery to straightaway join us at the table.

Henry stopped in mid-sentence. He was obviously about to ask this stranger what the hell he thought he was doing, barging in on a private conversation. As Henry eyes met the stranger's, however, Henry performed a perfect double take and exclaimed, 'Leo?!'.

Closer inspection, indeed, revealed the stranger to be none other than the missing Leo the Lover himself. The reason for the temporary loss of recognition was Leo's state of dress. He invariably wore a T-shirt, shorts and thongs, day in and day out, irrespective of the weather or the occasion. This incarnation had shoes, long trousers and a coat and tie.

'Aha!' said Henry. 'You've obviously been in trouble with the law and you've been to court.'

Henry knew about courts. He had once been pinched for knocking off oysters from a public lease and had managed to get himself acquitted by buying a new suit and appearing to be respectable when he fronted the magistrate.

'That's just the sort of comment I'd expect from you, Henry,' said Leo. 'In fact I've been to a funeral in Canberra. I always get dressed up for funerals. It's my way of showing respect for the dead; something I'll even do for you, probably one day soon.'

'How was the train trip down and back?' asked Henry, ignoring the jibe. 'Seems like the train must have been a little late, eh?'

'Don't get me started!' said Leo defensively. 'I had to drive down, and I'll tell you why: there are now only *two trains a day* going to and from Canberra. It's a disgraceful situation when you think about it. That railway links Australia's largest city to the national capital. No other country in the world would allow it.

'Besides, if I had caught the train I would have missed my nightly session here at the club. And, even though I love to travel by train, there is a limit to what a man can sacrifice for a train ride.'

It seemed that Leo was wound up and in a talkative mood. Henry commented later to me and Backhoe Bill, who was with us at the table, that it was probably because Leo hadn't been able to talk during the funeral service and was making up for it now.

'Speaking of railways,' Leo said, looking at Henry the Hun, 'I've got a trivia question for you. When is a railway station a church?'

None of us knew what he was talking about and we must have shown it by our blank looks. This seemed to give Leo great satisfaction and, before Henry the Hun could think up a reply, Leo continued: 'It's when it's the Anglican church at Ainslie in Canberra, and that's where the funeral was today.

'It seems,' Leo went on, 'that the church was originally built in Sydney, at Rookwood Cemetery to be precise. When it was there, however, it was a railway station. You see, it was the terminus for the cemetery line.'

'Is that what they mean by "the end of the line"?' asked Henry the Hun, who never liked to see Leo complete a story without a few decent interruptions.

Leo ignored Henry. 'In the 1800s they used to bury people much more than they do now. They didn't have crematoriums so they had to have lots of cemeteries. When they established the cemetery at Rookwood it was too far out of the city for bodies to be taken there in the old horse-drawn hearses. It would have taken them a couple of days to get there.'

'But it was still the dead centre of Sydney, so to speak,' put in Henry. It was an old joke and no one laughed.

Ignoring Henry again, Leo continued. 'It was only natural they'd build a branch line into the cemetery, and funeral trains were in common use back then.

'So, at the end of the line they built a station out of sandstone that was shaped like a church. It had angels with trumpets carved on the arches. It even had a bell tower with bells that tolled when the funeral train pulled in. At the Sydney end they built another sandstone station, which you can still see today. If you look on the left-hand side as you're pulling into Central you can see it. It's called the Mortuary Station.

'There used to be a couple of trains a day during the week, so you can see it was a pretty popular trip. The coffin carriage could hold up to thirty coffins and the passengers, first and second class, rode in the front of the train accompanied by the undertakers.

'The trains also picked up at some of the stations on the way. When they reached Rookwood, people would take their dear departed to where the freshly dug graves were waiting. The length of the graveside eulogy depended on how far the grave was from the station.'

'How so?' asked Backhoe Bill, who seemed to be getting quite interested.

'Well, the train ran to a strict timetable and it took time to get the coffins to the more distant parts of the cemetery. So, the further away the grave was, the shorter the service had to be. Otherwise, you'd miss the train back and be stuck out there among the ghosts until the next day.'

'How do you know all this, Leo?' asked Backhoe.

'Ahh, good question,' said Leo, obviously feeling pleased with the attention he was getting. 'When the motor hearses took over from the trains they had no use for the old sandstone chapel at Rookwood. In fact the branch line was disconnected when it was cut by a new road. But, as it was shaped like a church, the Anglicans took a fancy to it. They bought it for the princely sum of a hundred pounds, took it apart block by sandstone block, and rebuilt it at Ainslie where it's now used as a church – All Saints Anglican Church.

'And I happen to know a lot about it because that's where I've been today, at an old mate's funeral. There's a lot of the history of it down there in the church, old photos and so on. And I reckon,' added Leo, 'it's

'The Anglican Church bought the station for £100 and moved it stone by stone to Canberra.' The opening of All Saints Church of England, Ainslie, 1957. NSW SA

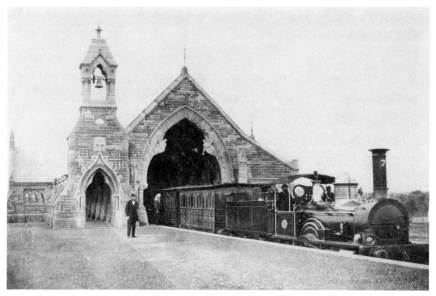

'At the end of the line they built a station that was shaped like a church.' NSW SA

good to see it used for the purpose it was built for, not just used for landfill or to build some yuppie's retaining wall.'

'All I can say,' said Henry the Hun, 'is that it was lucky it was built of solid sandstone. If it hadn't been sandstone, the walls might have collapsed when you walked into the church. I bet the last time you were in a church was when you were christened.'

As Leo ignored Henry yet again, Backhoe Bill, who continued to show a deal of interest in the topic, again chimed in: 'Yeah, you know those cemetery lines used to be quite common – I've even travelled on one meself.'

'Aw, cut it out Backhoe,' said Henry. 'We all know that you're carrying a bit of weight for your age, but you can't be that old. Don't tell me you were around before they had motor hearses?'

Now it was Backhoe Bill's turn to ignore Henry. 'Up in Newcastle,' he explained, 'the line that took people to Sandgate Cemetery didn't close until about 1985 and I went on it once with my mum to visit my grandmother's grave. It hadn't carried coffins for donkey's years but lots of people used it when they wanted to take flowers out to the cemetery and weed gravesites. On Mother's Day those trains were always packed.'

Henry the Hun was feeling a little left out of the conversation, so it was not surprising when he re-entered the fray. 'My Great Uncle Charlie lived in Newcastle,' he said. 'He reckoned there was a funeral tram that met the train as well.'

'I never heard of a funeral tram,' said Backhoe.

'Well, there was one,' Henry asserted, 'and it caused a few problems for undertakers, too. They had to have a few more skills than they have today. Because the body was often laid out in the house, the undertaker also had to book the hearse tram – and here's where the skill came into it. He had to make sure the coffin was carried down to the tram stop at just the right time. It wouldn't do to be waiting too long on the roadside with a coffin, a bunch of mourners and a funeral director in a top hat. It was pretty poor form to be early and a disaster to be late. It was pretty uncomfortable in wet weather, too.

'Evidently the hearse tram had plumes on each of its corners and space for two or three coffins at the back, and the mourners rode in the front of the tram.'

'Well, there are some great stories about the funeral *trains*,' said Leo, determined to be the expert of the day. 'One time, this old lady's coffin had been placed in the train when the undertaker was approached by her daughter. She explained that her mum had always wanted her to have her rings as a keepsake, but when they laid her out they had forgotten to remove them.

'The undertaker told the daughter not to worry and, when he had seen that all the mourners were aboard, he hopped into the coffin car with a screwdriver. By the time the train reached the cemetery, he had retrieved the rings and nobody was any the wiser. The daughter was very grateful. Even though everyone was sworn to secrecy, the word soon got around and that undertaker became a minor celebrity in his profession.'

'Just because he climbed into a coffin car and retrieved some rings?' scoffed an unimpressed Henry.

'No, you dill,' Leo replied. 'He became a celebrity because he was the only person ever to ride in the coffin carriage of a funeral train with a return ticket!'

'I might need an undertaker myself soon,' said Henry dryly. 'With all this talk a man could die of thirst. You'd better get yourself over to the bar and get a couple of drinks. You might be all dressed up fit to kill, but it's still your shout ...'

## THE MORTUARY TO ROOKWOOD CEMETERY LINE

By 1860 Sydney's population had expanded to the point where a general cemetery was needed. Some 80 hectares were gazetted for the purpose in an area that was then beyond the existing suburbs, near Haslems Creek Station on the railway line to Parramatta. This became Rookwood Cemetery.

A branch line into the centre of the cemetery was completed at the end of 1864 and funeral trains ran regularly from 1867. Leaving from the old Sydney Station twice a day at 9.15 am and 3.00 pm, the funeral trains stopped just short of Haslems Creek Station and backed along the branch line to the two cemetery platforms.

Having funerals operate from normal railway platforms at Sydney Central soon proved unsuitable. Funeral groups were forced to mix with commuters and a place was also needed to store coffins that arrived by train from the outer areas so, in 1869, the colonial architect, James Barnet, designed two church-like sandstone buildings, one at the Sydney end (which became known as the Mortuary Station) and the other at the cemetery.

Mortuary Station still stands today between Central and Redfern stations, which is quite close to the site of old Sydney Station near Regent and Devonshire streets.

The building at the cemetery end was 38 metres by 16 metres and the arch was 17 metres high. The trains backed right in and coffins were unloaded inside the building, which was decorated with angels holding scrolls and trumpets, to represent Judgment and Resurrection.

In the early twentieth century, funeral trains were made up of six of the most basic carriages in operation at the time. Between Mortuary Station and Rookwood they could be flagged down at any station to pick up coffins and funeral groups. At Homebush there was a long stop for ticket collection from the living passengers; coming back the trains again stopped at Homebush for tickets to be checked and to make a list of where people needed the train to stop on its journey back to Sydney.

In April 1948 the last funeral train ran and the branch line was closed. Motor vehicles had made the service unnecessary and a new road was planned which cut the branch line and made it impractical to operate.

In 1957 the building at the Rookwood end was purchased by the Anglican Church for the grand sum of £100 and moved stone by stone to Canberra. It still stands as All Saints Church of England, in the suburb of Ainslie.

'The Mortuary Station still stands today between Central and Redfern stations.' RH

# SAVED BY A CIGARETTE

*by Russell Hannah & Jim Haynes*

Australians have always had a habit of giving names to their trains.

Trains like 'the Indian Pacific' and 'the Ghan' that traverse the continent are famous around the world. In addition, there was 'the Spirit of Progress' and 'the Southern Aurora', the names given to the services that joined Sydney and Melbourne, while 'the Overland' still links Melbourne and Adelaide. Queensland had 'the Sunlander' to Cairns, 'the Inlander' from Townsville to Mount Isa, 'the Westlander' to Charleville, and its unique 'Gulflander', which travels over the most remote and isolated line in Australia, between Normanton to Croydon in the Gulf Country. Western Australia has its 'Prospector' to Kalgoorlie and 'the Australind' to Bunbury; Victoria its 'Vinelander' to Mildura; and New South Wales had 'the Silver City Comet' to Broken Hill, the world's first air-conditioned train.

Some regular commuter trains acquired names from the travellers who rode them and the staff who worked them. Some of these became official, like 'the Fish', 'the Chips' and 'the Heron' that brought workers from the Blue Mountains to Sydney every weekday. They carried their names proudly on their sides and on their locos, and were regarded with great affection by their regular passengers.

Other names remained unofficial. The Wollongong to Sydney commuter train was known as 'the Silver Slug', while the little train that carried fruit from the orchards of north-west Sydney became 'the Apricot Express'.

The commuter train that left Mount Victoria in the heart of the Blue Mountains at 6.09 am every weekday morning was christened 'the Slogger' by some of the passengers who travelled on it regularly from the mountains. It was due into Central at 8.32 am and, consistent with its name, it generally delivered its human cargo fairly close to time. Just a handful started the trip at Mount Victoria but, after stopping at almost all the stations in the mountains, its passenger complement was often swollen to well over 600, many of them standing, by the time it left Parramatta.

It was no fancy train, just an old workhorse of eight wooden carriages, close to retirement, hauled by an electric loco. Certainly not the sort of train you'd expect people to be talking about for years to come. Yet, on Tuesday 18 January 1977, at 8.13 am, the Slogger tragically crashed its way into history.

You see, the Slogger was the train involved in the nation's worst ever railway accident, and the second worst peacetime disaster on Australian soil – what Australians call 'the Granville Disaster'.

A couple of kilometres east of Parramatta, Bold Street crosses the main railway line at Granville. The Bold Street Bridge was supported by two concrete-buttressed steel trestles, each with eight steel stanchions. The bridge had been opened in 1956 and had been constructed by the Department of Railways.

Significantly, the concrete slab that made up the deck of the bridge was not poured for six months after the support structures of the bridge had been completed. This was because the local council was responsible for the approaches to the bridge and these were not completed at the time. When the council came to finish the bridge, it was found that the profile of the approaches differed markedly from what the railway engineers had assumed. The difference in the levels was made up by pouring an additional thickness of concrete onto the bridge deck. Although this was undoubtedly safe under normal conditions, it meant that the weight of the bridge deck was twice that of its original design.

## THE Sun ✳ says

# GRANVILLE
# JAN 18, 1977

**IT TOOK only seconds yesterday for an important political issue to become a major human tragedy.**

Sydney's emergency services — and thousands of ordinary people — — reacted magnificently to the disaster at Granville.

The NSW Government also acted with welcome speed in launching two inquiries.

Those inquiries may or may not determine the precise cause of the Granville train crash.

But a third inquiry is also essential.

This must determine whether a long-neglected, rundown railway system is being asked to do too much.

Early last year, the warnings of a railway disaster were coming from experts of all kinds, including the present Minister for Transport, Mr Cox.

In office, Labor has acted on its election promises by ordering new signalling equipment, new double-decker carriages and stepping up maintenance work.

But there is a gap between the best railway intentions and good results.

Even with more money, years would be needed to make the system modern and safer.

Until then, there must be a thorough investigation of the safety standards of the whole system as it is — not as we would like it to be.

'Some regular commuter trains acquired names … like "the Heron".' NSW SA

Just prior to passing under the bridge from the west, the railway line takes a long left-hand curve and passes over a set of points. Following the disaster, close examination revealed that the line's gauge had widened as a result of pressure from the heavy traffic on the line as it curved; some of the dog spikes that were used to hold it in place were badly worn. This had not been detected by maintenance staff. It was a derailment waiting to happen, but nobody foresaw just how potent and deadly this combination of circumstances would be.

That morning in January 1977, the Slogger left Parramatta Station and quickly built up to its maximum allowable speed of 80 kilometres an hour. As it rounded the curve and crossed over the points approaching the Bold Street Bridge, the driver, Ted Olencewicz, heard a loud crack and, at the same time, the engine left the rails. Olencewicz applied the emergency brake, but it was too late. The loco began to rock and roll sideways and upwards. Then it hit the trestles of the bridge, taking out eight of the sixteen steel stanchions. Having demolished the stanchions, the loco passed under the bridge, dragging the first and second carriages off the rails with it as it went.

As it did this, the engine also hit a steel mast that was holding the overhead electric wires and broke it off at the base. The mast swung out like a great sword and sliced the top off the first carriage. It was like opening a tin of sardines. Eight people lost their lives and thirty-four were injured in the first car.

By now the train had come to rest, and massive damage had been done. The first carriage was a disaster area. The second carriage was off the rails, with minor injuries sustained by its passengers. The other six cars were all still on the rails, however. All the guard in the rear carriage knew was that the train had stopped suddenly and he had been thrown off his feet.

What had occurred to this point was, unfortunately, merely act one of this terrible event. The rear of the third carriage and the front of the fourth carriage had come to a halt under the bridge. Apparently no one in these carriages was hurt in the derailment, though many were badly shaken by the train's abrupt and shaky halt.

For a full twenty seconds, it seemed that the worst was over – nothing happened. Then the unimaginable happened. The bridge began to sag.

The support for the bridge had been so seriously weakened that its weight could no longer be sustained and, seconds later, the whole northern span of the Bold Street Bridge, with its double load of concrete, crashed onto the third and fourth carriages. In all, 255 tonnes of concrete crashed into the old wooden carriages of the train. There was no resistance. The carriage sides were split asunder and their roofs were pushed down to within centimetres of the floor. The result was catastrophic. Those in the sections of the carriages under the bridge had no chance of survival or escape.

Forty-four of the seventy-seven passengers in carriage three lost their lives, and thirty-one of the sixty-four passengers in carriage four also died. The final count was eighty-three killed and 213 injured.

Within minutes, one of the greatest rescue efforts in Australia's history was under way. Police units, the Rescue Squad, ambulances, the fire brigade, medical teams from nearby hospitals, railway workers and a large number of volunteers quickly poured onto the scene of the tragedy.

Two of the first people to arrive were Chicka Thompson and Tony McGregor. They were fitters from the Clyde Railway Workshops who'd just finished a night shift and were having a couple of beers in the bar of the Granville Hotel, a pub that opened early to cater to shift workers. They heard what they later described as 'this bloody great bang' and ran across the footbridge and down the embankment to start pulling people from the wreckage of the train.

Chicka saved a young sixteen-year-old girl in the first carriage who had cut an artery in her arm. She was in shock and just stood staring at the spurting blood. Chicka tore a leather thong from around his neck and staunched the blood with a tourniquet. He then helped her through the carnage to the first of the St John's Ambulance men who were beginning to arrive.

Meanwhile, Tony had rushed to help the people in the crushed front section of the fourth carriage. He later told *The Bulletin*: 'I was talking to an old guy who seemed to be jammed between two seat cushions. He looked like he was pretty comfortable. As a matter of fact he said to me, "I reckon I've got a pretty soft possie here, mate". I was giving him a smoke when I saw him just staring at me, and I realised he was dead. When Chicka came back he reckoned I was bawling like a baby.'

There were many others like Tony and Chicka who heard the noise and were helping people before the main body of rescue teams arrived.

The concrete slab, however, was just too heavy to lift. It had to be cut up with jackhammers and removed in pieces using huge cranes. There was a constant danger that the rest of the bridge would collapse but rescue workers ignored this in the quest to find survivors and recover bodies. It was ten hours before the last of the injured was released from the wreckage, and the last of the bodies was not recovered until 3.20 pm the following day, thirty-one hours after the bridge came down.

There were many amazing stories to emerge from the Granville Disaster. There were tales of courage, tales of suffering, tales of endurance and stoicism, and tales of luck – both good and bad. Bob

'The first carriage was a disaster area: eight people lost their lives and thirty-four were injured . . .' NSW SA

Brain lived to tell such a tale. His is one of remarkable chance circumstances. It is also probably the only good news story about cigarette smoking to emerge in the last forty years.

Bob was thirty-four years old at the time and worked as an accountant in the city. Every morning he'd catch the bus from his West Guildford home to Parramatta Station and then take the train to Central. He often travelled with his friend Chris, who caught the same bus and train.

The Slogger was Bob's preferred train because, after Parramatta, it stopped only once, at Strathfield, which made it the quickest way of getting to work. Of course, it meant that he usually didn't get a seat, as the commuters who'd boarded the train in the mountains had already taken these, but Bob didn't mind standing. The only alternative was the slower suburban rattler that stopped at many of the intermediate stations. So, whenever he could, Bob always made an effort to catch the

'It was ten hours before all the injured were released and the last of the bodies was not recovered for thirty-one hours.' NSW SA

mountain train. As the third carriage stopped near the entrance to the platform, that was the one he always travelled in.

The morning of Tuesday 18 January 1977 began like any other for Bob. The only difference was that his mate Chris had had a bit of a stressful morning and hadn't had time for his morning cigarette. 'What about we get on the first carriage for a change?' Chris suggested, desperate for a smoke.

Back in 1977 smoking was allowed in some carriages on State Rail trains. Not in car three of the Slogger, but it was permitted in car one.

Bob agreed and they made their way to the front car. As the train was pretty full, they didn't manage to get a seat, so both stood at the rear of the car and Chris managed to light up his smoke. This change to their routine not only meant they weren't in the carriage that suffered the most fatalities – car three – but also by chance they were standing in what was to be the 'safest' end of the first carriage.

Bob recollects hearing the bang as the train left the rails. He remembers the carriage rocking to the left about 30 degrees then rocking to the right at about the same angle. At this point he recalls falling onto the floor and having Chris fall over on top of him.

The accountant's next memory is of waking on a stretcher beside the line with an ambulance man wiping blood from his face. His mate Chris was there as well. Bob's main concern was for his briefcase and the work papers he had in it – he kept asking Chris to go back and see if he could find it.

Not until much later that day did Bob become aware of the extent of the disaster. Fortunately, his injuries were not life threatening, though he still carries a legacy of Granville in the form of a damaged spine. He was hospitalised and had nine weeks off work due to his injuries. It was only when Bob saw the photographs in the following day's newspaper that he realised how lucky he was: if he had travelled in car three as he usually did, his chance of survival would have been almost zero.

Once his mind had cleared sufficiently for him to think back over the events of that morning, Bob realised what it was that had saved him. His mate Chris had wanted to have a smoke on the train. A cigarette saved Bob Brain's life. When he got out of hospital, the first thing he did was to buy Chris the largest carton of cigarettes he could find.

Strangely enough, Bob has since discovered that he is allergic to cigarette smoke – and he's eternally grateful that he didn't know about his allergy before that Tuesday in January 1977. For years afterwards, according to Bob, Chris drove his car to work rather than catch a train. He himself is still very sensitive to any strange bumps or swaying when he is travelling by train.

And as for the bridge, well, they rebuilt it over the twelve months following the disaster. One thing that the new design doesn't have is a stanchion supporting the centre of the span. In fact, since Granville, all bridges across railway lines in New South Wales have been single spans with no central supports. They cost a lot more but no government would be game to indulge in that sort of cost cutting after the Granville Disaster.

On the night of Thursday 20 January 1977, over two and a half days after the disaster, the first passenger train to run since the accident crept through the crash site. It was less than a quarter full.

A commuter train now leaves Mount Victoria at 6.01 am each working day, just a few minutes earlier than the old Slogger. It's a modern, double-deck, electric, inter-urban train. It's air-conditioned and does the trip just fourteen minutes faster than the Slogger. Millions of commuters have used the service since the accident, and the Granville Disaster has now become more history and folklore than actuality for most Australians.

But for people like Bob Brain, his mate Chris, Chicka Thompson and Tony McGregor, and the others who were there, the event will always remain a real and vivid memory. And you can be sure about one thing: no one has ever referred to a train as 'the Slogger' since that fateful day in 1977.

# ON THE NIGHT TRAIN

*by Henry Lawson*

*Have you seen the bush by moonlight, from the train, go running by?*
*Blackened log and stump and sapling, ghostly trees all dead and dry;*
*Here a patch of glassy water; there a glimpse of mystic sky?*
*Have you heard the still voice calling – yet so warm, and yet so cold:*
*'I'm the Mother-Bush that bore you! Come to me when you are old'?*

The night train. DF

*Did you see the Bush below you sweeping darkly to the Range?*
*All unchanged and all unchanging, yet so very old and strange!*
*While you thought in softened anger of the things that did estrange?*
*(Did you hear the Bush a-calling, when your heart was young and bold:*
*'I'm the Mother-Bush that nursed you; come to me when you are old'?)*

*In the cutting or the tunnel, out of sight of stock or shed,*
*Did you hear the grey Bush calling from the pine-ridge overhead?*
*'You have seen the seas and cities — all is cold to you, or dead —*
*All seems done and all seems told, but the grey-light turns to gold!*
*I'm the Mother-Bush that loves you — come to me now you are old'?*

# FARE EVASION

*by Russell Hannah & Jim Haynes*

Despite all the electronic ticketing devices, fare evasion on the railways is probably as prevalent today as it has always been. In fact with the demise of station assistants, and even stationmasters, it is probably easier now to avoid paying your fare than ever before.

It's a phenomenon as old as the railways themselves, of course. If you manage to get caught these days, it can bring you a quite hefty fine but not a prison sentence.

It was different in Henry Lawson's day. Way back in 1891, when he was twenty-four years old, Lawson spent nine months working on *The Boomerang* newspaper in Queensland and he often wrote his column in rhyme.

One obstinate fare evader was immortalised by Lawson. According to Henry, who was after all merely recording the news in rhyme, the fellow also copped a little more than he bargained for:

*A passenger travelled from Indooroopilly*
*To Ipswich on Monday (the Advocate tells),*
*And he paid not his fare, which we fancy was silly,*
*Although it is greatly the fashion with swells.*
*He wasn't a swell, and the SM said to him:*
*'You'll pay, or retire to quod if you don't.'*

*Then up to his full height the passenger drew him,*
*And plainly and flatly remarked, 'No I won't!'*
*'The constable then,' said the SM, 'must take yer.'*
*The constable came, and the sinner turned pale.*
*'I'll go,' said the man; said the peeler; 'I'll make yer!'*
*And then marched the passenger off to the gaol.*

For those not conversant with the slang of the day, a 'peeler' is, of course, a policeman (like 'bobby', named after Sir Robert Peel, the British prime minister and founder of the Irish Constabulary), while 'quod' was slang for prison (an abbreviated form of 'quadrangle').

Back in Lawson's time those who engaged in the art of fare evasion were said to be 'scaling the trains' (or trams). It was, however, quite common, especially during the depressions, to 'jump a rattler'. This simply meant hoisting your swag into a stationary or slow-moving goods train and hoping that no railway police, who were specially employed to prevent such abuses, would discover you.

Unemployed travellers and itinerant workers began 'jumping the rattler' in the Depression of the 1890s but the practice became much more widespread in the Great Depression of the 1930s because of a catch 22 situation regarding 'susso' payments to the unemployed. In the Great Depression men had to work for 'relief', or susso. Many of the nation's roads were originally built and bituminised by relief workers in the 1930s. If there was no such work available, they were obliged to look for work somewhere else. Unemployment relief was only available for a limited time in one place, then men had to move on to show they were attempting to find work – they could not go on receiving relief in the same town.

As they had no money for fares (relief was in the form of rations and coupons), the men often tried to jump the rattler in order to move on and thus meet the requirements of unemployment relief benefits. When they did this they were breaking the law and were fair game for the railway police or, in rural areas, the regular police force, who performed the task of upholding the law as it applied to rail travel. The local copper thus had ready access to cheap labour to chop the station firewood and perform manual labour and repairs to police property and dwellings.

There were two notorious railway cops during the 1930s Depression, both of whom were the terror of swagmen and rattler jumpers. One of these was 'Wingy, the Railway Cop', so called because he only had one arm, and the other was the notorious Sergeant Small.

Small probably became more famous than any of the others because of his alleged habit of pretending to be a hobo and tricking any swagman who was on a train into revealing himself. He also had a reputation for unnecessary violence.

Tex Morton immortalised Sergeant Small in a song, which had the distinction of being the first song to be banned from radio airplay in Australia when Small's family complained about it being a slur on a man who was only doing his job. In the song Morton accused the railway cop of entrapment. According to Tex, Sergeant Small would pretend to be a rattler jumper himself by walking alongside stationary goods trains and asking if there was 'any room in here'; once a place was offered, he would arrest the men and make them chop firewood, and even on occasions beat them up.

Booking and ticketing staff at Sydney Central, circa 1900. ARHS NSW RRC

When the family threatened legal action against Tex's record company, Regal Zonophone, for libel, the record company was forced to recall the records and Tex recorded a far less specific version of the song. But many people say that the real Sergeant Small lived in Queensland, and Tex got it wrong – and there are quite a few different versions of this song, some set in Queensland and some in northern New South Wales. In the Queensland folk version, the singer wishes he 'was twenty stone and all of seven foot tall' so he could 'take a special trip up north and beat up Sergeant Small'. The sergeant whose family was upset about the song actually lived in Quirindi in northern New South Wales.

There were many ingenious ways of avoiding paying your fare, and the most common involved doing it in the relative comfort of a passenger compartment, rather than the dirt and discomfort of a goods van. Hiding in the toilet was a favourite, but any ticket inspector worth his salt would lie in wait if the 'engaged' sign was up. Eventually the scaler would have to come out.

The following story is a favourite among Kiwis living in Australia.

It seems that there were six friends, three New Zealanders and three Australians, who worked in Wagga and decided to catch the South West Mail up to Sydney to watch an Australia–New Zealand Test match. When they got to the station, the Aussie blokes noticed that the Kiwis only bought one ticket between the three of them.

'How are the three of you going to travel on just one ticket?' asked one of the Aussies quizzically.

'Watch and you might learn something,' said one of the Kiwis.

Well, they boarded the train and the journey began. As soon as they saw the inspector enter the carriage, the three Kiwis headed straight for the toilet and crammed into it. The inspector checked the Aussies' tickets and noticed that the 'engaged' sign was showing on the toilet door. He banged on the door and in his most authoritative voice said, 'Tickets, please.'

The toilet door opened about a centimetre, just enough to push the ticket through. The inspector clipped the ticket and moved on.

The Australians were greatly taken by this and thought it was most clever, especially for New Zealanders. They decided that they would do the same on the return trip.

When they arrived at Central for the return trip, the Aussies bought one ticket between them but the Kiwis bought three platform tickets at a penny each. Again, the Aussie blokes were quite perplexed by it all. Perhaps we should mention that Australia had won the Test, so the Kiwis were rather despondent, not too happy with Australians in general and in a mood for revenge.

'How are you three going to travel without any ticket at all?' asked one of the Aussies.

'Watch and you might learn something,' replied one of the Kiwis.

The train pulled out and after a while one of the Kiwis said, 'I think the inspector's coming through.'

The Aussie trio had been keeping an eye on the toilet to make sure it wasn't occupied when they needed it. Now they made a beeline for the cubicle in order to be ensconced before the inspector came through.

After a sufficient break of about ten minutes, one of the Kiwis got up, strode purposefully down the carriage, stood outside the cubicle that all three Aussies were crammed into, and called out, in a most authoritative voice, 'Tickets, please.'

# A FREE RIDE

*by Russell Hannah & Jim Haynes*

'Have you seen Dobbin Walsh today, Henry?' asked Leo the Lover.

Henry the Hun was rather taken aback by this abrupt question. He had just joined the table and hadn't even taken a sip from his first beer.

Dobbin works at the Coal Loader and Henry's job has nothing to do with loading coal, or loading anything else for that matter, so it was unlikely he'd have seen Dobbin Walsh during the day.

Sensing that something was afoot, Henry said, 'No, should I have?'

'Just thought you might have,' said Leo enigmatically. 'There was a bit of an incident down at the loader this morning. Dobbin called in earlier and has been telling everyone about it. They're all talking about it, so I thought you might have heard.'

Leo seemed well and truly primed to tell him the story, so Henry asked the inevitable question: 'Why, what happened?'

'Well,' said Leo, launching into the story, 'it appears Dobbin was a bit early for work this morning. I know it's unlike him but he had to get a lift into work with a mate because his car was at the panel beaters having rust cut out. His mate apparently dropped him at the turn-off to the loader and he walked the rest of the way.'

'It'd be the first time for twenty years that Dobbin's walked that far,' interrupted Henry. 'It must be all of half a kilometre.'

'That's probably true,' Leo agreed, 'but if it hadn't been for Dobbin walking to work, there'd be one less poor bugger in the world today.'

'Strewth,' I said, 'you mean old Dobbin Walsh saved someone's life?'

'If you let me tell the story you'll find out,' Leo remarked, giving me one of his looks. 'It seems that Dobbin was walking across the road bridge that crosses the line, you know the one the coal trucks use, when a coal train passed under the bridge.

'Now, old Dobbin had a bird's eye view of the wagons and stopped to watch them pass below. Being so early, he was in no hurry to get to work.'

'They don't pay you any extra for going early,' philosophised Backhoe Bill, who had joined the table and was listening intently.

Determined not to be diverted from his story, Leo ignored the comment and continued. 'As Dobbin looked over the rail into the coal wagons, he noticed one that seemed to have a blanket or maybe it was a coat, lying on the top of the coal.

'When it passed right under him he could see it was actually a body lying on top of the coal. Dobbin figured that this bloke was either dead or unconscious.'

'Old Dobbin was always quick like that,' remarked Henry sarcastically.

'Well, either way,' continued Leo, 'Dobbin knew what would happen once the wagons reached the loader. Those wagons have trap doors underneath and they drive over a large hole above a big conveyor belt. As they pass over it, the trap doors open and the coal falls onto the conveyor belt; then it moves along the belt to the stockpile and gets loaded into ships and sent overseas, to Japan mostly.'

'A body wouldn't even be seen if it was mixed up in that process,' mused Backhoe Bill.

'Dead right,' said Leo. 'And Dobbin's worked at the loader for twenty years so he knows that. He also knows that time is of the essence, so he goes as fast as he can, which isn't very fast at all, to stop the train before it empties its human cargo.'

'And he made it in time?' I asked.

'Seems he just got there in time,' said Leo. 'The wagon with the body in it was only three away from emptying out when Dobbin stopped the train.'

'So Dobbin's a hero, eh?' said Backhoe, shaking his head. 'There's hope for us all.'

'Was it a live body or a dead body?' asked Henry rather bluntly.

'It turned out that the body was very much alive. When they climbed up into the wagon and woke the body up, it turned out to be suffering from a monumental hangover and was clutching an empty flagon.'

'Ah, I'm starting to think I know how he got there, too,' said Henry.

'And you'd be right,' said Leo. 'The train was bringing its coal down from Lithgow and it seems this bloke had a very big day in the Lithgow pubs. When the pub near the railway closed he'd bought himself a flagon and looked for a nice, quiet place to drink it. Evidently he went into the rail yards and climbed up into one of the coal wagons. There was no loco attached to it, so he assumed it wasn't going anywhere.

'Bad luck for him, because that coal was destined for Port Kembla. Halfway through the night a loco was attached and he was on his way.

Coal ready for Japan. RH

Of course he was dead to the world and too drunk to know what was happening.'

'He was bloody lucky to come out of that alive,' said Henry, thoughtfully. 'It'd have to be a billion-to-one chance that Dobbin Walsh would ever be early for work, and even another billion-to-one chance that he could move fast enough to stop the train. What did they do with the bloke?'

'Well,' said Leo, 'apparently someone called the police, and they were none too sympathetic. There's talk that they are going to charge him with a number of offences,' Leo chuckled and counted on his fingers for emphasis. 'Trespass is one, then illegal drinking on a train, travelling without a ticket, and causing a public mischief. But whatever they charge him with, it's better than the alternative.'

'Yeah,' laughed Henry the Hun, 'the alternative would be to come back from Japan as part of a Toyota Corolla.'

'Trust you to think of that,' said Leo. 'All this talk has made me thirsty – I suppose I'll have to shout.'

Leo resupplied the table and returned to his seat.

'You know,' said Backhoe Bill, 'I've been thinking.'

Leo raised his eyebrows but restrained himself. We all waited for Backhoe Bill's words of wisdom.

'I've talked to a few blokes who used to jump the goods trains in the old days and they all reckoned wheat trains were the best to travel on. They'd certainly be a bit more comfortable than lying on lumps of coal.'

'You wouldn't be able to do that today,' said Leo. 'All the wheat trains have covers over them.'

'But they didn't years ago,' Backhoe countered. 'They used to have tarpaulins over the wagons, but you could pull those back and burrow into the wheat a bit. You'd just leave your head poking out. They reckon it was like a first-class sleeper. It was especially warm during winter.'

'You'd have to be careful not to go to sleep on a wheat train,' said Henry. 'Otherwise you might come back as a chelsea bun.'

Henry's attempt at humour got a polite chuckle from me, but no one else laughed.

Henry was, however, obviously warming up and getting into storytelling mode himself. 'Did I ever tell you how my Great Uncle Alex always travelled on trains without a ticket?' he asked.

'Not *another* great uncle,' growled Leo. 'How many great uncles have you got?'

'Well, if they were all alive, I'd have twenty-five,' said Henry proudly. 'My grandparents came from large families – in fact my father had one gross of first cousins.'

Leo was silent and I assumed he was doing some quick mathematics to see if he could catch Henry out telling porkies. Henry sipped his beer.

'I suppose it's possible to have a hundred and forty-four first cousins if your family do nothing else except fornicate and raise children,' he remarked after a pause.

'They were all good Catholics,' grinned Henry. Then he continued his tale.

'Great Uncle Alex had a very short career on the railways. He met a girl from Perth when she was visiting Sydney and reckoned he'd follow her back when she went home. Great Uncle Alex always was a bit of a romantic. He scrounged around and got the train fare to Perth, then wrote to this girl and told her he was coming and asked her if she could meet him at the station.'

'Did they meet up?' I asked, hoping for a fairy-tale ending.

'Well, she met him at the station all right but she had a bloke with her. Evidently she said, "Hello Alex; this is my fiancé, Bill."'

'Ohh dear …'

'Exactly,' said Henry, 'and Great Uncle Alex was a pretty perceptive bloke. He was quick to get the hint that perhaps he shouldn't hang around. But anyway, there he was, stuck in Perth with no money and with nowhere to live. So, he did the only reasonable thing a young bloke could do in those days. He joined the railway.'

'There was always plenty of work on the railways in those days,' said Backhoe Bill.

'Must have been,' remarked Leo dryly, 'you worked on the railway back then, didn't you?'

Henry hurried on before the conversation took a turn for the worse. 'There was lots of work,' he said, 'but most of it was out in the bush, and that's where they sent Great Uncle Alex. They gave him a rail pass to Northcliffe, a few hundred kilometres south-west of Perth.'

'Nice country down there,' Backhoe added.

'Yes, and Uncle Alex thought the job would be a featherbed 'cos there were only two or three trains a week, but he was in for a shock. Apart from the summer heat and the flies, he had to lay sleepers by hand, with only a sledgehammer and a crowbar. To top it off, the ganger was a real bastard and when he kicked my uncle up the arse after a fortnight in the job, Uncle Alex jobbed him and then, of course, he had to leave the job.'

'They obviously needed a backhoe to move those sleepers,' said Backhoe Bill.

'They don't do anything by hand these days,' replied Henry. 'They've got great hulking machines to lay and replace sleepers. It was much tougher in the old days.'

'What did your uncle do then?' I asked, just to get the story back on track.

'Well, he had to get back to Perth so he could get back to Sydney,' Henry went on. 'So he got to the marshalling yards in Bunbury. It was night, and he was looking for a goods train that might be going to Perth. One of the problems with jumping rattlers was that you didn't know where the hell they were going.'

'That much of your story is true anyway,' Leo put in. 'It was a lucky dip where you'd end up.'

'Anyway, there he was, looking for a likely train, when he heard a voice say, "Get your head down, ya mug, or someone'll see ya."

'Uncle looked around and couldn't see where the voice was coming from. "Get down, ya mug," the voice hissed again, "or you'll cruel it for me as well."

'"Where are you?" whispers my Uncle Alex, as loud as he dares.

'"Over here in the fruit wagon – where are you going?" says the voice,

'"Perth!" says Uncle Alex.

'"Well, that's where this train's going in fifteen minutes. Jump in here with me, but keep your bloody head down," says the disembodied voice.

'So, Great Uncle Alex climbed into that fruit wagon and that's how he met one of the most famous travellers in Australian railway history,' Henry declared with pride. 'You see, Uncle Alex had met up with Timetable Scottie.'

'Timetable Scottie!' exclaimed Leo. 'I've heard of him. He was famous years ago – I think there was a story about him in *The Australasian Post* magazine.'

'Probably was,' said Henry. 'Timetable Scottie knew everything about everything on the Australian railways. He knew where you could expect to find every loco; he knew how long it took to travel between stations. He knew when was the best time, and best place to get on and off goods trains. Best of all, he knew exactly where every train – passenger or goods – was going and what time it would arrive, allowing for lateness of course.'

'Is that fair dinkum?' asked Backhoe Bill.

'My oath,' replied Henry. 'He was an amazing man. Every Railway Department in the country should have paid him thousands of dollars and got him to organise their timetables. Trouble was, they could never find him. He'd never paid a fare in his life and reckoned he'd travelled on every line in the country.

'By the time that goods train reached Perth, Great Uncle Alex knew more tricks about rail travel than any other bloke in the country. Timetable Scottie was indirectly responsible for Great Uncle Alex becoming the wealthy man he is today.'

'Don't tell me that you actually have someone *wealthy* in your family,' said Leo the Lover. 'This Great Uncle Alex must be the black sheep of the clan.'

'As you've heard, he wasn't always wealthy,' said Henry patiently. 'I'll tell you how Timetable Scottie's advice got him on the road to wealth and respectability.'

'This'll be good,' Leo murmured.

'Months later, Great Uncle Alex was doing it tough – no money, no job and stuck in Hay. The temperature over a century every day and flies in plague proportions. Great Uncle Alex wanted to head for the coast but he had no money for a fare. That's when he used a trick that Timetable Scottie had taught him.

'He went down to the station and told the stationmaster he was looking for a job on the railways. In those days there was plenty of work on the railways but everyone had to do a written test. The stationmaster explained that Uncle Alex would have to go to Sydney to do the test. So, the stationmaster wrote him out a rail warrant, and off went Uncle in style.

'When he got to Sydney he did the test and he went pretty well in it. Great Uncle Alex was no dill. The last part of the test was for colour blindness. You can't get a job on the railways if you're colourblind, for obvious reasons. Every time they put a card in front of Uncle Alex and asked him what he saw, he said he saw brown dots. No matter what colour they flashed before him all he saw was brown dots.

'So they asked Uncle Alex to wait outside, and a few minutes later one of the examiners came out and told him that, even though he'd done exceptionally well in the test, they were unable to employ him 'cos he was colourblind. Uncle Alex pretended to be devastated and bunged on a blue.'

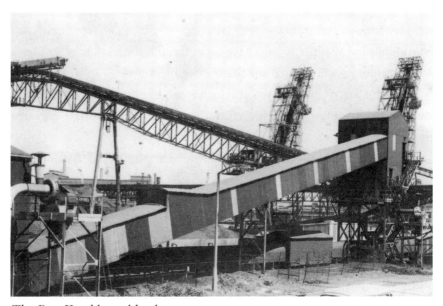

The Port Kembla coal loader. RH

'You mean to say he saw brown, then pretended to see red, and bunged on a blue?' asked Leo, with a deadpan face.

'He sure did,' Henry asserted. 'He claimed that he'd been brought to Sydney under false pretences, that it had cost him heaps of money, and he was now stuck in an expensive city with no money. He put on such a turn that they offered him a rail warrant to anywhere that he wanted to go in New South Wales, just to quieten him down.'

'That's a good trick,' laughed Backhoe Bill. 'Where did he want to go?'

'Uncle Alex thought the North Coast sounded a nice spot to spend the summer,' said Henry. 'So he ended up with a ticket to Murwillumbah, the end of the line north.'

'That's a nice place,' I ventured. 'I was born up that way many years ago. How did Uncle Alex become wealthy?'

'He took the old North Coast Mail and got a job on a banana plantation. Then he courted the owner's daughter and married her. When the old fellow died he inherited the plantation. Now he owns six or seven plantations. He's on the local council and he's the biggest banana grower on the Tweed.'

'And all this because he met Timetable Scottie, eh?' mused Leo the Lover.

'Of course,' said Henry. 'If he hadn't got that free ticket to Murwillumbah, his life would have been far different. He may still have been jumping goods trains, just like Timetable Scottie.'

'Do you know how to tell if bananas are legitimate or not?' It was Backhoe Bill speaking. He sometimes seems to come from a different dimension.

'No,' Leo replied patronisingly. 'How do you tell if bananas are legitimate?'

'You put them in a string bag and all the bastards fall out,' said Backhoe Bill.

'Backhoe, that's even worse than Henry's attempts to be funny,' said Leo the Lover. 'You'd better get yourself over to the bar and shout – we all deserve a drink after that.'

# UPPER OR LOWER ...
# A LITTLE DRAMA

*Anon*

Dramatis personae:

FARMER FRED: *a Queensland cocky attempting to buy a ticket to Townsville at his local railway station*

STATIONMASTER SMITH: *an over-officious rural stationmaster*

The scene: *the ticket window of a rural railway station somewhere in Queensland*

STATIONMASTER SMITH: *Next, please!*

FARMER FRED: *Townsville return, please.*

STATIONMASTER SMITH: *That's an overnight train, sir. Sleeper?*

FARMER FRED: *Ahhh yes ... yes please.*

STATIONMASTER SMITH: *Upper or Lower berth, sir?*

FARMER FRED: *Ahhh, is there a difference?*

STATIONMASTER SMITH: *Of course there is a difference.*

FARMER FRED: *Ahhh ... what's the difference?*

STATIONMASTER SMITH: *There's a difference of seventy cents.*

FARMER FRED: *Why's that?*

STATIONMASTER SMITH: *The Lower is higher than the Upper.*

FARMER FRED: *Eh?*

STATIONMASTER SMITH: *The higher price is for the Lower.*

FARMER FRED: *Eh?*

STATIONMASTER SMITH: *If you want a berth Lower, you'll have to go higher.*

FARMER FRED: *What?!*

STATIONMASTER SMITH: *We sell the Upper lower than the Lower. In other words, the higher, the lower.*

FARMER FRED: *Why?*

STATIONMASTER SMITH: *Most people don't like the Upper — although it is lower on account of it being higher.*

FARMER FRED: *Ehh?!*

STATIONMASTER SMITH: *When you occupy an Upper you have to get up to lie down and get down when you get up.*

FARMER FRED: *Errrrr ...?*

STATIONMASTER SMITH: *You can have the Lower if you pay higher. The Upper is lower than the Lower because it is higher. If you're willing to go higher, it'll be lower!*

FARMER FRED: *Awwww ... blimey! Forget the sleeper, I'm getting giddy already. How much to sit up all night?*

'When you occupy an "Upper" you have to get up to lie down and get down when you get up.' RH

# THE FLYING GANG

*by A.B. 'Banjo' Paterson*

*I served my time, in the days gone by,*
*In the railway's clash and clang,*
*And I worked my way to the end, and I*
*Was the head of the 'Flying Gang'.*
*'Twas a chosen band that was kept at hand*
*In case of an urgent need;*
*Was it south or north, we were started forth*
*And away at our utmost speed.*
*If word reached town that a bridge was down,*
*The imperious summons rang —*
*'Come out with the pilot engine sharp,*
*And away with the flying gang.'*

*Then a piercing scream and a rush of steam*
*As the engine moved ahead;*
*With measured beat by the slum and street*
*Of the busy town we fled,*
*By the uplands bright and the homesteads white,*
*With the rush of the western gale —*
*And the pilot swayed with the pace we made*
*As she rocked on the ringing rail.*
*And the country children clapped their hands*

*As the engine's echoes rang,*
*But their elders said: 'There is work ahead*
*When they send for the flying gang.'*

*Then across the miles of the saltbush plain*
*That gleamed with the morning dew,*
*Where the grasses waved like the ripening grain*
*The pilot engine flew –*
*A fiery rush in the open bush*
*Where the grade marks seemed to fly,*
*And the order sped on the wires ahead,*
*The pilot must go by.*
*The Governor's special must stand aside,*
*And the fast express go hang;*
*Let your orders be that the line is free*
*For the boys in the flying gang.*

'There is work ahead when they send for the flying gang.' The Flying Gang
crew with their train decorated for Federation 1901. ANU NB

# TO THIRROUL

*by D.H. Lawrence (adapted from* **Kangaroo***)*

### D.H. LAWRENCE IN AUSTRALIA

David (D.H.) and Frieda Lawrence arrived in Fremantle, WA, in early May of 1922 and had moved on to Sydney by the end of the month. They rented a cottage in the mining village of Thirroul, south of Sydney, for the bulk of their three-month stay in eastern Australia. It was there that Lawrence wrote the entire first draft of the novel *Kangaroo* in a period of six weeks; he later revised the manuscript while he and Frieda were staying in Mexico, on another leg of their journey.

The novel is strongly autobiographical: the hero, Richard Somers, and his wife, Harriet, are Lawrence and Frieda thinly disguised. The cottage rented by the Lawrences at Thirroul was called 'Wyewurk', and he used the exact same name for the cottage visited by the Somers and their neighbours in the novel. The account of the train trip from Sydney to Thirroul was obviously based on trips Lawrence took to and from Sydney by train while living at Thirroul. The observations of the scenery, and Australian life of the time, are exceedingly accurate and perceptive.

The only thing Lawrence altered in the novel was the name of Thirroul: he called it 'Mullumbimby'. We have taken the outrageous liberty of using the name 'Thirroul' in this edited extract, for two reasons. Firstly,

Lawrence's detailed use of the town as the village in the novel is very well historically documented and obvious. Secondly, as there is an actual town of Mullumbimby very differently located in the far north of New South Wales, we feel that Australian readers will find the extract makes more sense that way.

Somers could feel waves of friendliness coming across the hedge.

'Isn't it a lovely evening again?' Victoria called to him as he stood on the summer-house top.

'Very lovely. Australia never ceases to be a wonderland for me, at nightfall,' he answered.

'Aha!' she said. 'You are fond of the evening?'

He had come down from his point of vantage, and they stood near together by the fence.

'He's late tonight, is he?'

'Yes. He said he might be. Is it six o'clock?'

'No, it's only a little after five.'

'Is it? I needn't be expecting him yet, then. I always miss Jack so much when the evening comes, and he isn't home. You see I was used to a big family, and it seems a bit lonely to me yet, all alone in the cottage. I do miss my family. We were six of us all at home together, and it makes such a difference, being all alone.'

'Was your home in Sydney?'

'No, on the South Coast – dairy-farming. No, my father was a surveyor, so was his father before him. Both in New South Wales. Then he gave it up and started this farm down south. Oh yes, I liked it – I love home. I love going down home. I've got a cottage down there that father gave me when I got married. You must come down with us some time when the people that are in it go. It's right on the sea. Do you think you and Mrs Somers would like it?'

'I'm sure we should.'

'And will you come with us for a week-end? The people in it are leaving next week. We let it furnished.'

'We should like to very much indeed,' said Somers.

They went to Thirroul by the two o'clock train from Sydney on the Friday afternoon, Jack having managed to get a day off for the occasion. He was a sort of partner in the motor-works place where he was employed, so it was not so difficult. And work was slack.

Harriet and Victoria were both quite excited. The Somers had insisted on packing one basket of food for the house, and Victoria had brought some dainties as well. There were few people in the train, so they settled themselves right at the front, in one of those long open second-class coaches with many cane seats and a passage down the middle.

'This is really for the coal-miners,' said Victoria. 'You'll see they'll get in when we get further down.'

It came on to rain, streaming down the carriage windows. Jack lit a cigarette, and offered one to Harriet. She, though she knew Somers disliked it intensely when she smoked, particularly in a public place like this long, open railway carriage, accepted, and sat by the closed window smoking.

The train ran for a long time through Sydney, or the endless outsides of Sydney. The town took almost as much leaving as London does. But it was different. Instead of solid rows of houses, solid streets like London, it was mostly innumerable detached bungalows and cottages, spreading for great distances, scattering over hills, low hills and shallow inclines. And then waste marshy places, and old iron, and abortive corrugated iron 'works' – all like the Last Day of creation, instead of a new country. Away to the left they saw the shallow waters of the big opening where Botany Bay is: the sandy shores, the factory chimneys, the lonely places where it is still bush. And the weary half-established straggling of more suburbs.

'Como', said the station sign. And they ran on bridges over two arms of water from the sea, and they saw what looked like a long lake with wooded shores and bungalows: a bit like Lake Como, but oh, so unlike. That curious sombreness of Australia, the sense of oldness, with the forms all worn down low and blunt, squat. The squat-seeming earth. And then they ran at last into real country, rather rocky, dark old rocks, and sombre bush with its different pale-stemmed dull-leaved gum-trees standing graceful, and various healthy-looking undergrowth, and great spiky things like yuccas. As they turned south they saw tree ferns standing on one knobbly leg among the gums, and among the rocks ordinary ferns and small bushes spreading in glades and up sharp hill-slopes. It was virgin bush, and as if unvisited, lost, sombre, with plenty of space, yet spreading grey for miles and miles, in a hollow towards the west. Far in the west, the sky having suddenly cleared, they saw the magical range of the Blue Mountains. And all this hoary space of bush between. The strange, as it were, *invisible* beauty of Australia, which is undeniably there, but which seems to lurk just beyond the range of our white vision. You feel you can't see – as if your eyes hadn't the vision in them to correspond with the outside landscape. For the landscape is so unimpressive, like a face with little or no features, a dark face. It is so aboriginal, out of our ken, and it hangs back so aloof. Somers always felt he looked at it through a cleft in the atmosphere; as one looks at one of the Aborigines with his wonderful dark eyes that have such an incomprehensible ancient shine in them, across gulfs of unbridged centuries. And yet, when you don't have the feeling of monotony in landscape, you get a sense of subtle, remote, *formless* beauty more poignant than anything ever experienced before.

'Your wonderful Australia,' said Harriet to Jack. 'I can't tell you how it moves me. It feels as if no one had ever loved it. Do you know what I mean? England and Germany and Italy and Egypt and India – they've all been loved so passionately. But Australia feels as if it had never been loved, and never come out into the open. As if man had never loved it, and made it a happy country, a bride country – or a mother country.'

'I don't suppose they ever have,' said Jack.

'But they will?' asked Harriet. 'Surely they will. I feel that if I were Australian, I should love the very earth of it – the very sand and dryness of it – more than anything.'

'Where should we poor Australian wives be?' put in Victoria, leaning forward her delicate, frail face – that reminded one of a flickering butterfly in its wavering.

'Yes,' said Harriet meditatively, as if they had to be considered, but were not as important as the other question.

'I'm afraid most Australians come to hate the Australian earth a good bit before they're done with it,' said Jack. 'If you call the land a bride, she's the sort of bride not many of us are willing to tackle. She drinks your sweat and your blood, and then as often as not lets you down, does you in.'

'Of course,' said Harriet, 'it will take time. And of course a *lot* of love. A lot of fierce love, too.'

'Let's hope she gets it,' said Jack. 'They treat the country more like a woman they pick up on the streets than a bride, to my thinking.'

'I feel I could *love* Australia,' declared Harriet.

'Do you feel you could love an Australian?' asked Jack, very much to the point.

'Well,' said Harriet, arching her eyes at him, 'that's another matter. From what I see of them I rather doubt it,' she laughed, teasing him.

'I should say you would. But it's no good loving Australia if you can't love an Australian.'

'Yes, it is. If as you say Australia is like the poor prostitute, and the Australian just bullies her to get what he can out of her and then treats her like dirt.'

'It's a good deal like that,' said Jack.

'And then you expect me to approve of you.'

'Oh, we're not all alike, you know.'

'It always seems to me,' said Somers, 'that somebody will have to water Australia with their blood before it's a real man's country. The soil, the very plants seem to be waiting for it.'

'You've got a lurid imagination, me dear man,' said Jack.

'Yes, he has,' said Harriet. 'He's always so extreme.'

The train jogged on, stopping at every little station. They were near the coast, but for a long time the sea was not in sight. The land grew steeper – dark, straight hills like cliffs, masked in sombre trees. And then the first plume of colliery smoke among the trees on the hill-face. But they were little collieries, for the most part, where the men just walked into the face of the hill down a tunnel, and they hardly disfigured the land at all. Then the train came out on the sea – lovely bays with sand and grass and trees, sloping up towards the sudden hills that were like a wall. There were bungalows dotted in most of the bays. Then suddenly more collieries, and quite a large settlement of bungalows. From the train they looked down on many many pale-grey zinc roofs, sprinkled about like a great camp, close together, yet none touching, and getting thinner towards the sea. The chimneys were faintly smoking, there was a haze of smoke and a sense of home, home in the wilds. A little way off, among the trees, plumes of white steam betrayed more collieries.

A bunch of schoolboys clambered into the train with their satchels, at home as schoolboys are. And several black colliers, with tin luncheon boxes. Then the train ran for a mile and a half, to stop at another little settlement. Sometimes they stopped at beautiful bays in a hollow between hills, and no collieries, only a few bungalows. Harriet hoped Thirroul was like that. She rather dreaded the settlements with the many many iron roofs, and the wide, unmade roads of sandy earth running between, down to the sea, or skirting swamp-like little creeks.

The train jogged on again – they were there. The place was half-and-half. There were many tin roofs – but not *so* many. There were the wide, unmade roads running so straight as it were to nowhere, with little bungalow homes half-lost at the side. But they were pleasant little bungalow homes. Then quite near, inland, rose a great black wall of mountain, or cliff, or tor, a vast dark tree-covered tor that reminded Harriet of Matlock, only much bigger. The town trailed down from the foot of this mountain towards the railway, a huddle of grey and red-painted iron roofs. Then over the railway, towards the sea, it began again in a scattered, spasmodic fashion, rather forlorn bungalows and new 'stores' and fields with rail fences, and more bungalows above the fields, and more still running down the creek shallows towards the hollow sea, which lay beyond like a grey mound, the strangest sight Harriet had ever seen.

Next to the railway was a field, with men and youths playing football for their lives. Across the road from the football field was a barber's shop, where a man on horseback was leaning chattering to the barber, a young intelligent gentleman in eyeglasses. And on the broad grass of the

'The train jogged on, stopping at every little station.' WCL

roadside grew the trees with the bright scarlet flowers perching among the grey twigs.

Going towards the sea they were going away from the town that slid down at the bush-covered foot of the dark tor. The sun was just sinking to this great hill face, amid a curdle of grey-white clouds. The faintest gold reflected in the more open eastern sky, in front. Strange and forlorn, the wide sandy-rutted road with the broad grass margin and just one or two bungalows.

The sea roared loudly, but was not in sight. Next along the forlorn little road nestled a real bright red-tiled roof among a high bushy hedge, and with a white gate. 'I do hope it's that,' said Harriet to herself. She was so yearning to find another home.

'Is that it?' said Harriet timidly at last, pointing to the bright red roof.

'Yes, that's it,' said Victoria, pleased and proprietary.

Harriet followed eagerly on Jack's footsteps across the road. She peeped over the white gate as he unfastened it. A real lovely brick

'The train jogged on again – they were there.' NSW SA

house, with a roof of bright red tiles coming down very low over dark wooden verandahs, and huge round rain-tanks, and a bit of grass and a big shed with double doors. Joy! The gate was open, and she rushed in, under the tall, over-leaning hedge that separated them from the neighbour, and that reached almost to touch the side of her house.

A wooden side verandah with bedsteads – old rusty bedsteads patched with strip and rope – and then grass, a little front all of grass, with loose hedges on either side – and the sea, the great Pacific right there and rolling in huge white thunderous rollers not forty yards away, under her grassy platform of a garden. She walked to the edge of the grass. Yes, just down the low cliff, really only a bank, went her own little path, as down a steep bank, and then was smooth yellow sand, and the long sea swishing up its incline, and rocks to the left, and incredible long rollers furling over and crushing down on the shore. At her feet! At her very feet, the huge rhythmic Pacific.

How the sea thundered!

Harriet liked the house immensely. It was beautifully built, solid, in the good English fashion. It had a great big room with dark jarrah timbering on the roof and the walls: it had a dark jarrah floor, and doors, and some solid, satisfactory jarrah furniture, a big, real table and a sideboard and strong square chairs with cane seats.

Through the open seaward door, as they sat at the table, the near sea was glimmering pale and greenish in the sunset, and breaking with a crash of foam right, as it seemed, under the house. If the house had not stood with its little grassy garden some thirty or forty feet above the ocean, sometimes the foam would have flown to the doorstep, or to the steps of the loggia. The great sea roaring at one's feet!

The sun rose golden from a low fume of haze in the north-eastern sea. The waves rolled in pale and bluey, glass-green, wonderfully heavy and liquid. They curved with a long arch, then fell in a great hollow thud, and a spurt of white foam and a long, soft, snow-pure rush of forward flat foam.

'The train came out on the sea, lovely bays with sand and grass and trees.' NSW SA

The Lawrences (left of picture) at their Thirroul cottage with friends. WCL

There was an unspeakable beauty about the mornings, the great sun from the sea, such a big, untamed, proud sun, rising into a sky of such tender delicacy, blue, so blue, and yet so frail that even blue seems too coarse a colour to describe it, more virgin than humanity can conceive; the land inward lit up, the prettiness of many painted bungalows with tin roofs clustering up the low up-slopes of the grey-treed bush; and then rising like a wall, facing the light and still lightless, the tor face, with its high-up rim so grey, having tiny trees feathering against the most beautiful frail sky in the world. Morning!

# IN A WET SEASON

*by Henry Lawson*

It was raining – 'general rain'.

The train left Bourke, and then there began the long, long agony of scrub and wire fence, with here and there a natural clearing, which seemed even more dismal than the funereal 'timber' itself.

The only thing which might seem in keeping with one of these soddened flats would be the ghost of a funeral – a city funeral with plain hearse and string of cabs – going very slowly across from the scrub on one side to the scrub on the other. Sky like a wet, grey blanket; plains like dead seas, save for the tufts of coarse grass sticking up out of the water; scrub indescribably dismal – everything damp, dark, and unspeakably dreary.

Somewhere along here we saw a swagman's camp – a square of calico stretched across a horizontal stick, some rags steaming on another stick in front of a fire, and two billies to the leeward of the blaze. We knew by instinct that there was a piece of beef in the larger one. Small, hopeless-looking man standing with his back to the fire, with his hands behind him, watching the train; also, a damp, sorry-looking dingo warming itself and shivering by the fire.

The rain had held up for a while. We saw two or three similar camps further on, forming a temporary suburb of Byrock.

The population was on the platform in old overcoats and damp, soft felt hats; one trooper in a waterproof. The population looked cheerfully and patiently dismal. The local push had evidently turned up to see off some fair enslavers from the city, who had been up-country for the cheque season, now over. They got into another carriage. We were glad when the bell rang.

The rain recommenced. We saw another swagman about a mile on struggling away from the two, through mud and water. He did not seem to have heart enough to bother about trying to avoid the worst mud-holes. There was a low-spirited dingo at his heels, whose whole object in life was seemingly to keep his front paws in his master's last footprint.

The traveller's body was bent well forward from the hips up; his long arms – about six inches through his coat sleeves – hung by his sides like the arms of a dummy, with a billy at the end of one and a bag at the end of the other; but his head was thrown back against the top end of the swag, his hat brim rolled up in front, and we saw a ghastly, beardless face which turned neither to the right nor the left as the train passed him.

After a long while we closed our book and, looking through the window, saw a hawker's turn-out, which was too sorrowful for description.

We looked out again while the train was going slowly, and saw a teamster's camp: three or four wagons covered with tarpaulins, which hung down in the mud all round and suggested death. A long, narrow man, in a long, narrow, shoddy overcoat and a damp felt hat, was walking quickly along the road past the camp. A sort of cattle-dog glided silently and swiftly out from under a wagon, 'heeled' the man, and slithered back without explaining. Here the scene vanished.

We remember stopping – for an age it seemed – at half-a-dozen straggling shanties on a flat of mud and water. There a rotten weatherboard pub, with a low, dripping verandah, and three wretchedly forlorn horses hanging, in the rain, to a post outside. We saw no more, but we knew that there were several apologies for men hanging about the rickety bar inside – or round the parlour fire.

Streams of cold, clay-coloured water ran in all directions, cutting fresh gutters, and raising a yeasty froth whenever the water fell a few inches. As we left, we saw a big man in an overcoat riding across a culvert; the tails of the coat spread over the horse's rump, and almost hid it. In fancy still we saw him – hanging up his weary, hungry, little horse in the rain, and swaggering into the bar; and we almost heard someone say, in a drawling tone: ''Ello, Tom! 'Ow are yer poppin' up?'

The train stopped (for about a year) within a mile of the next station. Trucking-yards in the foreground, like any other trucking-yards along the line; they looked drearier than usual, because the rain had darkened the posts and rails. Small plain beyond, covered with water and tufts of grass. The inevitable, God-forgotten 'timber', black in the distance; dull, grey sky and misty rain over all.

A small, dark-looking flock of sheep was crawling slowly in across the flat from the unknown, with three men on horseback zigzagging patiently behind. The horses just moved – that was all. One man wore an oilskin, one an old tweed overcoat, and the third had a three-bushel bag over his head and shoulders.

Had we returned an hour later, we should have seen the sheep huddled together in a corner of the yards, and the three horses hanging up outside the local shanty.

We stayed at Nyngan – which place we refrain from sketching – for a few hours, because the five trucks of cattle of which we were in charge were shunted there, to be taken on by a very subsequent goods train. The Government allows one man to every five trucks in a cattle-train.

We shall pay our fare next time, even if we have not a shilling left over and above. We had haunted local influence at Comanavadrink for two long, anxious heart-breaking weeks ere we got the pass; and we had put up with all the indignities, the humiliation – in short, had suffered all that poor devils suffer whilst besieging Local Influence. We only thought of escaping from the bush.

The pass said that we were John Smith, drover, and that we were available for return by ordinary passenger-train within two days, we think – or words in that direction. Which didn't interest us. We might have given the pass away to an unemployed in Orange, who wanted to go outback, and who begged for it with tears in his eyes; but we didn't like to injure a poor fool who never injured us – who was an entire stranger to us. He didn't know what outback meant.

Local Influence had given us a kind of note of introduction to be delivered to the cattle-agent at the yards that morning; but the agent was not there – only two of his satellites, a cockney colonial-experience man, and a scrub-town clerk, both of whom we kindly ignore. We got on without the note, and at Orange we amused ourself by reading it. It said: 'Dear Old Man – Please send this beggar on; and I hope he'll be landed safely at Orange – or – or wherever the cattle go, – Yours, –'

We had been led to believe that the bullocks were going to Sydney. We took no further interest in those cattle.

After Nyngan the bush grew darker and drearier, and the plains more like ghastly ocean; and here and there the 'dominant note of Australian scenery' was accentuated, as it were, by naked, white, ring-barked trees standing in the water and haunting the ghostly surroundings.

We spent that night in a passenger compartment of a van, which had been originally attached to old No. 1 engine. There was only one damp cushion in the whole concern. We lent that to a lady who travelled for a few hours in the other half of the next compartment.

The seats were about nine inches wide and sloped in at a sharp angle to the bare matchboard wall, with a bead on the outer edge; and the cracks having become well caulked with the grease and dirt of generations, they held several gallons of water each. We scuttled one, rolled ourself in a rug, and tried to sleep; but all night long, overcoated and comfortered bushmen would get in, let down all the windows, and then get out again at the next station. Then we would wake up frozen and shut the windows.

We dozed off again, and woke at daylight, and recognised the ridge gum-country between Dubbo and Orange. It didn't look any drearier than the country further west – because it couldn't. There is scarcely a part of the country out west which looks less inviting or more horrible than any other part.

The weather cleared, and we had sunlight for Orange, Bathurst, the Blue Mountains, and Sydney. They deserve it; also as much rain as they need.

# WHAT DO YOU MEAN, MEAN?

*by Russell Hannah & Jim Haynes*

'Were you born in a tent?' asked Leo the Lover.

Henry the Hun had just entered the club and left the door open again. Though the club had air-conditioning of a sort, it didn't work when the door was left open.

'If you wore proper clothes you wouldn't be whingeing about the cold,' Henry replied testily, going back to close the sliding door.

Leo was dressed as he always was. Sartorially elegant in T-shirt, shorts and thongs. Leo refused to make concessions to the weather or climate when it came to his wardrobe.

'It's spanner weather, all right,' Backhoe Bill interjected, cryptically.

'Spanner weather?' I asked, as it seemed someone was supposed to. 'What's that?'

'So cold it tightens your nuts,' answered Backhoe, who had a way with words at times.

I rarely intervene too much in the conversation in our corner at the club. I'm much happier to sit back and listen to the stories unfold. Today, however, I thought I'd make an uncharacteristic contribution to the topic in hand.

'Here's my little saying for feeling the cold,' I said.

'Cold as an Eskimo, gloomy and glum,

Cold as the hairs on a Polar Bear's bum,

Cold as charity, and by God that's chilly,

But not as cold as poor dead Billy.

'We used to say that when we were kids.'

'Well, some of us obviously had deprived childhoods,' Leo remarked, without looking up from his beer.

'The way you dress it must have been you,' commented Henry.

'Speaking of charity,' said Leo, completely ignoring Henry, 'I was talking to Slippery Anderson the other day. He tells me he's come up with a nice little scheme down at St Vinnie de Paul.'

Slippery Anderson is a used-car salesman who frequents the club. He once played footy for the town and was renowned for being very hard to tackle. Ever since he's been known as 'Slippery'. Some people believe the name's more appropriate for a used-car salesman than a footy player. He also has a reputation for having short arms and long pockets.

'Bloody hell!' Henry exclaimed. 'Only Slippery would try to rip off a charity! What's he up to now?'

'Well,' said Leo, 'you know Slippery's between wives at the moment? His third wife left him because he wouldn't give her enough money to buy clothes, or anything else for that matter. So, he has to do his own laundry, until he can find another woman silly enough to do it for him.'

'He should dress like you,' interrupted Henry, 'he'd have no problem with his laundry then.'

'He's a car salesman, you dill, he can't please himself about his attire like I can,' said Leo, disdainfully. 'He has to dress so that he looks prosperous, otherwise people would say, "Would you buy a used car from this man?" It's sort of like a uniform.

'Anyway, Slippery's not much good at washing and ironing shirts, and it was starting to affect his appearance. And that affected his car-selling performance.

'He had to send them to the laundry and, when he did, he found it cost him four dollars for each shirt. He regarded this as an unnecessary expense and it worried him considerably. That was until he hit upon the idea of donating his dirty shirts to St Vinnie's.'

'How would giving his dirty shirts away save him money?' asked Backhoe Bill. 'New ones would cost him a lot more than four bucks, even if he bought them in bulk.'

'He's not called Slippery for nothing,' replied Leo. 'You see, when you donate shirts to St Vinnie's they have a group of volunteers who wash and iron them before they put them on sale. So, what Slippery's been doing is going into St Vinnie's each week and buying his own shirts back. Now, if you buy more than three shirts at St Vinnie's, the shirts are only two dollars each. So, Slippery saves two bucks on each shirt.

'Not only that, the St Vinnie's women love him because he's such a good customer. He says he's thinking about asking one of them out. He's found out she's their champion washer and ironer.'

'Geez, he must be the meanest man that ever lived,' said Backhoe Bill, taking another sip of his beer.

'No!' said Henry the Hun emphatically. 'There was a bloke who would give Slippery a start and a hiding when it comes to meanness. My Great Uncle Ken told me about him. He worked with him on the railways.'

As Leo had done recently, I was starting to wonder about all these great uncles of Henry's. He seems to have more of them than anyone could possibly have, and almost all of them appear to have worked on the railways.

'His name was "Mean Mike McGann",' Henry continued, 'and he was a driver who had come through the Depression. Uncle Ken used to fire for him sometimes. "A real hard bastard" was how he described him. Not too many drivers and firemen liked him, but he was the best-dressed driver in the system.'

'Sounds like a used-car salesman,' Backhoe put in.

'He always turned up to start a shift looking really smart,' continued Henry. 'Sometimes he even wore trousers with a belt, and a shirt instead of the blue overalls that drivers mostly wore.'

'Doesn't sound like he was too mean with his money if he dressed like that,' challenged Leo.

'Ah! But he bought his clothes pretty cheaply,' returned Henry, who had wanted just that response from someone. 'You see,' he continued smugly, 'in those days, when they brought bodies into the morgue, they used to bury them in shrouds so they'd take off their clothes, launder them and sell them off. Of course, they were cheap. Very few people wanted to walk around in dead people's clothes. Mean Mike not only wore them, but he used to boast about where he got them from.'

'Strewth, that's a bit distasteful,' said Leo the Lover. 'Not even old Slippery would come at that.'

'There's a good story about Mean Mike's meanness,' said Henry.

'Well, share it with us, Henry,' I said. 'But let me get the beers before you start.'

When there was a fresh beer in everyone's hand, Henry took up the story.

'It seems my Great Uncle Ken was firing a late-night mail train out of Central. It was about eleven pm and his driver was Mean Mike.

'Before they even pulled out of Central, Mean Mike said he was starving hungry. So, he grabbed the banjo, took a couple of eggs out of his tucker box and proceeded to fry them in the fire.'

'Bet he didn't offer your uncle any either,' said Backhoe Bill.

'Mean Mike wouldn't have offered his own mother any, even if she hadn't eaten for a week,' exclaimed Henry.

'Hang on a minute,' I said. 'I know we've had this before – but what's a banjo again, and why was he frying eggs on it?'

'A banjo is a coal shovel, you dill,' said Leo the Lover, before Henry could answer. 'Drivers and firemen cooked their meals on a clean coal shovel in the open firebox – now stop interrupting.'

Henry paused while Leo put me right and then went on. 'Anyway, Mean Mike scoffed his eggs with a bit of toasted bread as they headed out of Central. But soon he turned pale ∴ and then he started to turn a bit green. Next thing, he was leaning out of the cabin, spewing his heart out.

'By this stage Uncle Ken was a bit worried. He decided Mean Mike was probably not fit for work and told him he should go home. Uncle

'A late-night mail train out of Central.' DF

Ken said he'd ring ahead for a replacement driver when they pulled into Strathfield.

'Mean Mike, however, assured him that everything was okay. Since he had offloaded the eggs he felt much better. Sure enough, according to Uncle Ken, Mean Mike seemed to have made a perfect comeback and was looking much improved. Uncle Ken assumed it was just a passing stomach complaint.

'When the train reached Valley Heights in the mountains, Mean Mike was evidently feeling a bit peckish again, so he grabbed the banjo and pulled out another couple of eggs. He followed exactly the same procedure – cooking the eggs and eating them. He didn't share any with Uncle Ken. Anyway, bugger me, within a few minutes, he's gone green again and before long he's leaning out of the cabin throwing up that lot of eggs.

'By now my uncle figured there must be something seriously wrong with Mean Mike. Maybe he had a duodenal ulcer or terminal stomach cancer. He reckoned that they should get a replacement driver as soon as possible, so Mike could go and see a doctor.

'But, once again, Mean Mike told my uncle he was quite okay. It was only the eggs that made him feel crook, he said. It was fine now; he didn't have any more eggs in his tucker box, so he'd be okay.

'Great Uncle Ken thought this was all a bit strange, but, as Mean Mike once again looked to have recovered, he decided not to insist on getting a replacement driver. "Do eggs always make you feel crook?" he asked Mean Mike.

'"Yeah," Mike replied, "I think I'm allergic to eggs."

'Well, my uncle was totally at a loss to understand why anyone would keep eating eggs if they knew they were allergic to them. You see, he had no idea just how mean Mean Mike was. But he found out when he asked, "Why do you keep eating 'em if you think you're allergic to them?"'

At this point Henry paused for a long sip of beer and Backhoe Bill came in on cue. 'What did Mean Mike say?' he asked.

Henry savoured the beer and the moment.

'Well, he looked at my Uncle Ken and said, "But Ken, I've got to eat 'em! You see ... I've got chooks!"'

'I've got to hand it to you, Henry,' Leo chuckled, 'Slippery's not in the race with that bloke.'

'Yeah, that's about the meanest thing I've ever heard of,' said Backhoe. 'To put yourself through all that because you're too mean to give your eggs away.'

'Yeah,' Henry agreed, 'and you could well fall into that category yourself if you don't get over to the bar and shout ...'

# GOING TO WOODY

*by Steele Rudd*

'On Boxing Day,' said Davidson, 'I sez to th' son, what about a run to Woody?'

Th' son, a returned soldier, had just come in from th' great far west, from:

'Out where the grinnin' skulls bleach whitely
Out where the wild dogs chorus nightly.'

'Just as you like,' sez he, and off we goes th' pair of us. We found a train at Eagle Junction, it wasn't waiting for us – we had waited an hour for it.

There is a junction there, but never an eagle hovering around that I could see, and never a person either whether the oldest or the youngest, or the most reliable or unreliable inhabitant, that ever saw one.

But that isn't a point in the tale at all if ye understand. The train was a long, long train, stuffed, packed, jammed as full of passengers as a bale of sheep's fleeces were of wool, or a barn of corn cobs were full of corn.

When it stopped to take us in, me and th' son ran up and down the platform, and about sixty others with baskets and bags and babies ran up and down it too. And while the porter with a stitch in his voice and humour in his eye shouted, 'Take your sits,' we ran up and down more an' more. Not a sit could we see to take. We couldn't even see into any of the carriages, though every window of 'em was down.

All we could see was walls of humans, humans, humans!

'It's no use Dad,' th' son sez, 'there's no room.'

'Not a bit of it, son,' sez I with a smile. He didn't understand. An' then I pulled open one of th' doors, and a lot of the freight fell out on to th' platform. Then he understood.

With a grin an' a good opinion of his old Dad, in he jumped over the top of two old chaps older than meself, lying on the platform with no coats or hats on 'em, an' so alarmed that they held fast to each other an' kept each other from rising. Then I forged in after him, pulled the door after me an' by holding me breath and putting a dint in me stomach managed to close it. Then the train went.

At Sandgate it stopped.

There me an' th' son wanted to get out. Every one in the carriage wanted to get out there, too, so they did. An' they were in such a tearing hurry that you'd think they were afraid the pubs an' the surf would go dry before they could get out an' get into 'em.

'Dammit!' I shouted, holdin' on for dear life: 'I'm not goin' to open this door if ye don't stop shovin' behind me! Didn't ye see what happened at Eagle Junction?'

But they hadn't seen anything. All they wanted to see, anyway, were the billows, an' the beers.

Just then, an obligin' porter pulled the door open all at oncet, and out went me an' th' son on to our heads draggin' a fat woman an' a couple of girls an' their boys and baggage along with us.

The rest of th' passengers poured out like cattle, tramplin' us and knockin' us down every time we tried to get up.

When we did manage to get up there were oranges an' sandwiches and cakes an' tea lyin' all about us, an' empty baskets belongin' to th' fat woman an' th' two girls.

We helped pick them up (th' oranges an' things I mean, not th' wimmen). Then we made for th' pier.

The pier is a great thing at Sandgate. There would be no Sandgate without it, and it's as far from the railway station as the railway station is from the swimmin' 'ole. The railway contractor ran out of material and had to stop work before he came to Sandgate or else things'd be different. They'll never be any different again I'm thinkin'.

All along by the pier were sunburnt city fishermen. All of them armed with rods and lines and knives and bags of bait an' wearin' terrible, determined looks. But none of them city fishermen never do have fish. But before they got home me an' th' son reckoned they'd have a few that weighed over 31 lb, not to mention the capture of a shoal of sharks as a by-product.

At the end of the pier there were a motor ship called the *Olivine* and a crowd of cautious, sea-faring folk hanging over the railings were lookin' down into her.

She rose an' bobbed about an' bunted the legs of the pier accordin' to the humour of th' waves, like a live ram on the end of a line.

So me an' th' son looked down into her, too. 'Are y' goin' across, Dad?' sez he. I didn't say anythin' for a while. There were a baby thunderstorm playin' round one end of the Bay that attracted me, so I took it into serious contimplation.

Then I cast me eye across to Woody, an' made a mental calculation, if y' understand, of the number o' knots there would be to swim in event of a Jonah bein' o' board. Also me mind dwelt awhile on ancient Bible history; when th' ships of Tarshish, as they called 'em, were shattered be an East wind.

Then I sez, 'Well, we ain't tom-cats, son, and can only die once, we'll go across,' an' down an' into th' cabin we goes. We went there because there was no room to stand or sit or lay our heads anywhere else without standin' or sittin' or layin' our heads on somebody else.

'All aboard!' yelled a sea-farin' voice. 'Stan' back!' Then the anchor was weighed an' off we went for Woody — the engine flickin' and pumpin'; other parts of the works thumpin' and jumpin'. Then swish! splash! heave! tosh! down! up!

An' damn if she didn't nearly go over, but changed her mind at th' last second!

'At Sandgate it stopped.' Sandgate Station, early twentieth century. BCC

'Look here, Dad,' th' son shouts, wobblin' about on his horseman's legs an' spittin' out salt water, 'by cripes I crossed over to France but never got a joy-ride like –' another mouthful of salt water shut him up.

Some of those on deck started singin' to keep their courage up. Just then a handsome young lady, from a shop-winder in Queen Street, who was rollin' in th' cabin along with me an' the son, began to look as pale as milk. She was with her boy an' was holdin' tight to him an' murmurin', 'How much further is it?'

All at once, th' ship reared an' made a sort of pig-jump, an' th' young lady was thrown out of her boy's arms into th' arms of th' son.

She held on to him an' he held on to her; an' she didn't seem to mind how long he had to hold on to her. So he didn't either.

When we reached the pier at Woody that baby thunderstorm was a ragin' gale, blowin' like blazes and spittin' lightnin'.

Like rats abandonin' a sinkin' ship, everyone left the *Olivine*, scrambled on to the pier and ran like emus for shelter. Then talk about

'The pier is a great thing at Sandgate. There would be no Sandgate without it ...' BCC

rain! Lawd, but it rained drops as large as grapes an' heavy as lead. Where to run for shelter me an' th' son didn't know no more than them who hadn't a berth booked in Noah's Ark.

But we ran with the others, and most of the others were lumberin' bags and baskets and some were tryin' to lumber others not so fleet of foot as themselves, and we all ran along the pier, and the harder and further we ran the heavier it rained and the wetter we got. Two beautiful little girls fell down, but no one had the leisure or the inclination to wait and pick them up.

When we reached the store verandah we were all drenched and soaked, and some of the girls looked as though they had not a stitch of clothes on at all!

But that verandah was very little good to us when we had reached it, we might as well have sat down on the pier an' taken it easy, f'r the storm was threatenin' to demolish it, anyway.

So into the store itself we swarmed, and into the tearooms; an' the last thing that me an' the son saw of it was a voice cryin' out of the wilderness of rain an' wind. 'Look at this! Oh look at this! An' yet our councillors refuse to build us a shelter shed here!' it said.

'When the winds abated,' said Davidson, 'an' the rain ceased, an' the calm came, me an' th' son an' all th' rest, like Noah an' his family leavin' the Ark, came out of the store, shook ourselves like wet dogs, picked our way through the rushing floodwaters, an' went to th' nearest pub, me an' th' son, I mean, not all the others.'

In 20 minutes the sun was out again an' it was blazin' hot, hotter than before th' blitherin' storm; the streets (that's the name they have for 'em) dried up, an' Boxing Day at Woody was itself agin … an' in full swing.

# THE GREAT TRIPLE R

## by *Russell Hannah & Jim Haynes*

### WOMEN ON THE RAILWAYS

Men seem to love trains. Quentin Crisp once commented that 'there is a relationship between men and machines similar to that between women and cats.'

Very few women feature in the stories we collected from railway workers. There is a good reason for this: for the first hundred years of its existence the railways employed very few women. Women didn't become train drivers, firemen, guards or stationmasters until relatively recently. True, some became gatekeepers and carriage cleaners but these were a relatively small proportion of railway workers.

Even today, with equal opportunity enshrined into our industrial awards, women still only make up a small proportion of the railway workforce. In New South Wales, for example, there are 2770 train drivers and only thirty-one of them are women. Of the 2070 track workers on the permanent way, only four are women.

Only in the area of station managers and assistants are there significant women workers. Here women are still under-represented, but make up 16 per cent of the workforce.

There was one area of the railways, however, where the workforce consisted predominantly of women. This was the catering department that flourished during the age of steam and spawned the great Railway Refreshment Rooms – the RRR.

For many decades 'the Great Triple R' was ruled over by those fearsome 'ladies in grey'. When the age of steam passed into history, the great era of country rail travel went with it. Sadly, the railway institution of the Railway Refreshment Rooms, and the women who worked them and ruled over them with a fist of iron, gradually faded into history also. Their story is worth telling.

Ever since human beings felt compelled to travel there has been a need to cater for their basic needs of food and accommodation. Hotels, inns and eateries are a part of every culture and feature in their oldest folklore and history.

In pre-railway days, travellers walked or rode. Fifty kilometres was a good distance to travel each day. In colonial Australia, shanties, pubs, boarding houses and roadside inns were scattered along the sides of the ill-formed roads.

The railways changed all that. A day's trip became little more than an hour and a week's journey could be compressed into a day. People still needed to be fed and accommodated, however, and a series of refreshment rooms grew up on Australian railway stations. In New South Wales alone, at the height of the steam era, there were over 120 such rooms scattered over the stations of the rail system.

The first NSW train rolled out of Sydney terminal on 26 September 1855. It went as far as Parramatta. Early growth was slow. By 1875 the lines had reached Gunning in the south and Kelso in the west, and another line stretched from Newcastle to Murrurundi in the north. Although these were reasonable distances, the need to build refreshment rooms into the stations was not a high priority for railway builders.

In fact, the famous engineer John Whitton, the man responsible for the enormous growth in the railway system up until 1890, was actively opposed to building refreshment rooms. It was a waste of precious resources, he said; all available money should go into building the lines.

# PRICE LIST.

| | | QUARTS | FLASKS | ½FLASKS |
|---|---|---|---|---|
| WHISKY | R·R·R· | 12·6 | 6·0 | 3·3 |
| ,, ,, | OTHER BRANDS EXCEPTING AUSTRALIAN | 12·0 | ,, | ,, |
| ,, ,, | AUSTRALIAN | 9·0 | | |
| BRANDY | | 12·0 | 5·6 | ,, |
| GIN OR SCHNAPPS | | 12·0 | | |
| RUM | | 10·0 | 4·6 | 2·6· |

| | | | PINTS | BABY |
|---|---|---|---|---|
| WINES AUSTRALIAN | 3·6 | | 2·0 | 1·0 |
| ALE | ,, ,, | 1·6 | | |
| LAGER & STOUT | ,, | | | |
| CHAMPAGNE | | PRICES ON ENQUIRY | | |
| LIQUEURS & SPECIAL LINES | ,, ,, | ,, | | |

| | | |
|---|---|---|
| SPIRITS | 9D | PER GLASS |
| RUM & AUSTRALIAN WHISKY | 7D | " " |
| ALE LAGER WINE &C | 6D | " " |
| AERATED WATERS | LARGE | 6D " " |
| ,, ,, | IF BOUGHT WITH BOTTLE | 3D EXTRA |

CIGARS  **R·R·R·** SPECIAL VALUE **6D** EACH

BOXES OF **50 £1·2·6**

ALL LEADING BRANDS OF TOBACCOS, CIGARS, AND CIGARETTES

AT SYDNEY PRICES.

'But what can people drink here when they are thirsty?' Refreshment rooms were eventually licensed. NSW SA

The official history of the NSW railways, published in 1955, tells us:

*The first refreshment room [at Sydney terminal] consisted of a counter and two stools. It was open only shortly before the departure and arrival of trains. Supplies were brought to the station by a kind old lady from her pastry cook shop in Botany Road. It was quite common to see hungry passengers anxiously looking out for Mrs Moon and her basket when she was a little later than usual.*

Despite Mrs Moon's recognition as the first purveyor of pastries at Sydney Station, other records indicate that that honour went to a certain Henry William Dudley, who initially operated out of a tent on some wasteland outside the station. His venture proved disastrous. The tent was constantly at risk of burning down due to cinders from the passing steam engines and, on one occasion, it blew away in a strong wind.

The early refreshment rooms were all leased out to private operators. Many of them did not seem to impress Railways Commissioner John Rae; in the early 1870s he wrote:

*There is no part of our railway economy so defective as the arrangements of the supply of refreshments to passengers. We are much behind our neighbouring colonies in this respect. When we turn to the railways in the mother country and on the continent, we find magnificent saloons ... They are placed under the control of Railway authorities; a tariff of prices guarantees the traveller from extortion; and the attendants being paid by salaries, no gratuities are expected or allowed.*

*In strong contrast with this, the keepers of what are facetiously called refreshment rooms on our Railways are little more than apple-stall holders, and vendors of lollipops and stale pastry, serving out junks of sandwiches and messes of tea and coffee to their customers, without any regard to their accommodation and comfort.*

Rae's vision was not to be achieved in total for another forty-five years or more. It was then, in 1917, that the NSW Government stepped in, took control of the previously leased refreshment rooms, and so created the Great Triple R. In the meantime an era of construction of refreshment rooms with attendant accommodation was commenced.

The two decades after 1875 were the grand era of New South Wales railway construction. In the first ten years alone, over 1600 kilometres of railroad were built. Grand stations, which incorporated state-of-the-art refreshment rooms, were built at Albury, Junee and Werris Creek.

One of the major complaints about the refreshment rooms in the 1870s was that they could not serve alcohol. The colony had a reputation for terrible drunkenness but the temperance lobby reigned supreme. They formed an unholy alliance with the publicans, who feared the competition, and the granting of liquor licences was delayed until 1884.

This enforced teetotalism seemed strange to European visitors. Frenchman Edmond la Meslee, assistant to the French consul, made a trip by train and coach from Melbourne to Sydney in 1878. Having dined at the refreshment room at Mittagong, la Meslee had this to say:

> Goulburn was far behind and we stopped at the Mittagong Station for dinner. Monsieur de Castelnau, my young pupil and I got out and entered the refreshment room. Here following the universal custom of such establishments everywhere in the world, we were served with such scorching hot broth that we had the greatest difficulty in swallowing it. Whilst we were attacking a fowl we hit upon the idea of sampling the wine of the country.
>
> 'Waiter! A bottle of Albury wine.'
>
> 'Sir, we are not licensed to sell any kind of alcoholic drink, whatever.'
>
> 'What!' cried Monsieur de Castelnau. 'What can people drink here then, when they are thirsty?'
>
> 'We have coffee, tea, lemonade, seltzer water ...'
>
> 'That stuff! Do you want to make yourself a laughing stock to the whole world?'

'Trains stopped at refreshment room stations at any hour of the day or night.' RH

> *'No sir, it's the same in every railway refreshment room in New South Wales: they are all run on strict temperance principles. It's a Government rule.'*
>
> *'But heavens, if it is warm people can't drink coffee or boiling hot tea. That would not be very refreshing?'*
>
> *'There is lemonade, gingerbeer …'*
>
> *'Never mind, how much is it?'*
>
> *And thereupon we ran to take our seats, the bell warning us that the train was starting again for Sydney.*

These experiences were hardly in line with Commissioner Rae's ideas for the refreshment rooms.

In 1915 a government report indicated that the rental received from refreshment rooms leases was £16 000. Expenditure on maintenance and depreciation was running at about £20 000 per year. At this time the government stopped renewing leases and took over the running of the refreshment rooms. By 1917 they controlled the thirty-eight major outlets.

Thus began the great era of the Great Triple R. Women were about to take their place as an integral part of the railway workforce. Nearly 80 per cent of the staff was female.

The government takeover was an immediate success. In the first twelve months of state control the refreshment rooms made a profit of £25 000. This rose to over £68 000 in 1920.

Women earned just under half the wages of men. Female waitresses on the railways earned 35 shillings per week. Their male counterparts picked up 75 shillings. Women were not classified as permanent workers and had no access to government superannuation, long service leave or sick pay.

Trains stopped at refreshment room stations at any hour of the day or night. Hours of operation for refreshment rooms were often something like 2.30 am to 4.30 am, followed by 7 am to 8.30 am; or 9 am to 11.30 am followed by 9.30 pm to 11.30 pm. Though the actual hours worked were the regulation eight, they were spread over twenty-one hours of the day.

'The refreshment room would revert to its usual somnolence until the next train.' NSW SA

'The war years produce some of the RRR's finest hours.' RRR Werris Creek staff during World War II. WC RMT

Many women lived in the railway accommodation and had compulsory deductions taken from their wages for meals and accommodation. This was a source of much discontent and, together with the irregular hours and broken shifts the women had to work, may have accounted for their legendary grumpiness.

Stories of the grumpy 'ladies in grey' abound. This one is typical:

RRR WAITRESS: *What do you want?*

WEARY TRAVELLER: *How about a cup of tea, a pie and a few kind words?*

RRR WAITRESS: *There's your tea. There's your pie. That's two and sixpence.*

WEARY TRAVELLER: *What about the few kind words?*

RRR WAITRESS: *Don't eat the pie!*

When the train pulled into the station, all hell broke loose as a trainload of hungry and thirsty passengers descended on 'the ref rooms'. They all had to be fed and refreshed within periods of time that ranged from ten to forty minutes.

Working the Great Triple R was a stressful occupation. When the train left, the staff had cleaning-up duties. Then the ref room would revert to its usual somnolence until the next train re-ignited the frantic activity.

In some places, passengers sat down to silver-service three-course meals in ornate dining rooms. Other stations just had fruit, pie and coffee stalls called 'tearooms'. The humble railway pie was certainly the fast food of the railway era.

It wasn't passengers' needs that made the Railway Refreshment Rooms such a great institution; it was the fact that trains used steam power. Steam locos needed to be changed, watered and re-coaled. This meant that long stops at some stations were inevitable.

These steam maintenance facilities were not necessarily in major towns. They were more likely at the junction of several railway lines. Thus the major refreshment rooms existed where there were significant loco yards. Werris Creek, for instance, a town devoted almost entirely to servicing the railway, had some of the most prestigious railway buildings in the state, including a magnificent refreshment room with overnight hotel-style accommodation. South Grafton – not Grafton City – was the major refreshment break on the North Coast, and at Junee the refreshment room was the showpiece of the system.

The war years produced some of the RRR's finest hours. Packed troop trains were a regular occurrence but troop movements were secret. The women of the RRR were often given just one hour's notice to feed up to 4000 men. During this time, assistance was provided by the Voluntary Aid Detachment. In the small towns like Gloucester, north of Maitland, the RRR and the VAD would service up to five troop trains a day. During the course of the war, they served over one million meals at that station alone.

Perhaps the finest hour of any refreshment room occurred during the floods of 1955 in Narrabri. Water was lapping over the platform and the surrounding area was one vast inland sea when the last train arrived in from Walgett. The passengers soon realised that they were trapped at the station. The refreshment room cooking facilities were still operational but there was a serious shortage of food supplies.

Jim Madigan, an earth-moving contractor from Gunnedah, who was on the train, would write:

> *The adaptability of people in an emergency was amazing. Two cows that were tethered near the station were brought onto the platform and milked to supply the babies and children amongst the crowd. Six sheep and a pig seen floating past still alive were rescued from the water only to be slaughtered. This meat plus a bag of potatoes consigned northwest from Narrabri were used to cook meals in the refreshment room facilities. During the first 48 hours of the flood the people stranded on the station were probably the best fed in the whole of Narrabri.*

In some places, passengers sat down to silver-service three-course meals in ornate dining rooms. ARHS NSW RRC

Around this time the RRR faced its greatest challenge, a challenge it could not survive. Steam power was being replaced by diesel power. Trains no longer needed lengthy stops, there was no need for re-coaling or loco changeovers. Prestige trains like the Southern Aurora and the Spirit of Progress as well as the Brisbane Limited and the various Daylight Expresses all carried on-board buffet or dining cars. The rise of road and air transport also meant that the catering services started losing money.

By the 1970s country passenger services had declined drastically. Roads and cars were much improved and speed seemed imperative to all journeys. The mail trains and most branch services had gone by the early 1980s.

These days, XPT services stop just long enough to disgorge their passengers and luggage, and pick up those who are boarding. A typical sight on railway stations today isn't passengers rushing for a coffee and pie at the refreshment rooms – it's smokers desperately

'Prestige trains like the Southern Aurora ... carried on-board buffet or dining cars.' RH

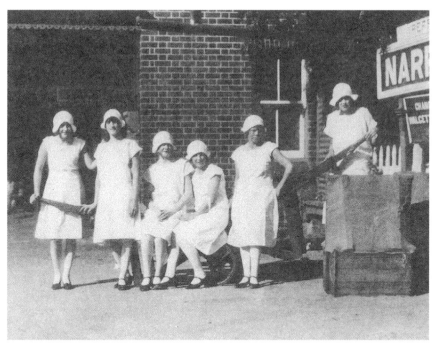

'The "ladies in grey" live only in memories and old photographs.' WC RTM

trying to finish their cigarette before being ordered back onto the non-smoking train.

With the end of the great age of rail travel, the Great Triple R closed down. Those that were kept were leased out to private operators. Commissioner Rae would have been devastated.

Many of the old buildings have been taken over by historical societies. Others have just become part of the station offices and buildings. Several, like the one at Glen Innes, in north-eastern New South Wales, retained their liquor licences and became pubs.

The refreshment rooms of today are the soulless roadhouses on our roads and freeways. No silver service there, no rush for the bar when the train pulls in, no good-natured chiacking as the crowd jostles its way to the counter, and, worst of all, no 'ladies in grey'.

The ladies in grey live only in memories and old photographs, but for fifty years they were an essential part of the great adventure of rail travel. Ahh, nostalgia is the child of progress ...

*When I was a boy my greatest joy*
*Was going away on a train.*
*In a corridor carriage my parents' marriage*
*Was lucky to stand the strain.*
*My brother and I would demand a meat pie,*
*Mum would wish on a star,*
*And Dad would say that he blessed the day*
*When they opened the Great Triple R.*

# TRIPLE R LADY

*by Jim Haynes*

*I'm a Triple R lady … you'll get no change from me,*
*Just pies and salad sandwiches and boiling cups of tea.*
*Don't think that you can jump the queue and if you push or shout,*
*I'll serve everyone but you … and you can just miss out.*

*'Cos you've only got ten minutes … then the engine gives a toot,*
*And if you end up hungry … I couldn't give a hoot,*
*You can't buy food back on the train and there's no dining car,*
*And you've got all night to travel to the next Triple R.*

*And the ladies there are just like me, tough and dressed in grey,*
*So if you want refreshments you'd best do things my way.*
*You can push and yell at me but I really wouldn't try it*
*'Cos if you do I'm warning you, you're going on a diet!*

*Be rude and I'll ignore you, be polite and I'll be cheerier,*
*'Cos I'm a Triple R lady … boss of the cafeteria,*
*If you dare annoy me, that's an easy thing to fix,*
*I've a hundred ways to sort you out, lots of little tricks.*

*Last time a bloke was rude to me, know what I did to him?*
*Gave him the hottest pie I had, filled his teacup to the brim,*
*And counted his change out slowly … so he'd run to*
*make the train,*
*Gee, that hot tea must have burned his hand,*
*he won't try that again.*

*For if the train begins to move it's you that has to worry*
*You want to catch the train, or wait for your change? I'm not in a*
*hurry.*
*I know which pies are cold and stale … it's easy to arrange it,*
*And once the train pulls out of here you can't come back to change it.*

*But when I'm in a good mood, I'm an angel dressed in grey,*
*I'll make your journey pleasant and brighten up your day,*
*'A nice hot pie? Of course love, and a nice hot cup of tea.'*
*But I'm a Triple R lady … so don't try to mess with me!*

*But just remember I'm the boss, this is my domain,*
*Your happiness depends on me when travelling by train.*
*With my sandwiches and drinks and cakes,*
*my pie rack and my urn,*
*I'm a Triple R lady, so stand and wait your turn.*

# CHASING THE TIN HARE

*by Russell Hannah & Jim Haynes*

'Did you see that?' asked Backhoe Bill.

Leo the Lover, of course, didn't see anything at all. Backhoe Bill was facing Leo and was looking at the TV set immediately above Leo's head.

Leo regards TV sets, loud poker machines, music and meat raffles as distractions. Leo believes that clubs are places where people should talk and tell stories and listen to stories, particularly his own. He also believes that this should happen in relative peace. The TV above his head is usually left on so that people in other parts of the bar can watch the races, football, boxing and cricket. When Leo is there, however, the sound is always turned off.

'You know, I'm not interested in anything that happens on TV, Backhoe, unless I'm watching it in the comfort of my own lounge room,' said Leo emphatically.

'Sorry,' said Backhoe Bill, realising he had breached protocol. 'I was just watching a dog race at Gosford and the lead dog was so fast that it caught the hare. I haven't seen that before.'

'Maybe it was a fast dog at that,' Leo replied, a little more gently. 'It's more likely, however, that the hare broke down.'

'I suppose you're right,' said Backhoe. 'I don't suppose that there would ever be a dog so fast that it could catch the old tin hare if it was working right.'

'I can tell you that there was one tin hare that no dog would ever catch if it was working right,' Leo chuckled cryptically. 'Though I caught it myself on many occasions ...'

Backhoe Bill looked puzzled. He should have known better, but he fell in. 'How on earth could you ever catch a tin hare at the dogs?' he asked.

Leo looked quite pleased with himself. 'I didn't say it was at the dogs, Backhoe; you weren't listening. What I said was that I caught the tin hare *on many occasions.*'

'Here we go,' sighed Henry the Hun, 'more railway stories.'

'I thought we were talking about greyhounds,' said Backhoe, more puzzled than ever.

'Tin Hares were the little rail motors that used to do passenger runs on country lines and non-electric outer suburban lines,' said Henry, attempting to steal Leo's thunder.

'Why were they called that, Leo?' asked Backhoe Bill. 'Did they hop along the rails?'

Leo wasn't sure whether Backhoe was having a go at him or just being stupid. You sometimes can't tell with Backhoe Bill. Still, it was too good an opportunity for Leo to let it pass. After all, it was another chance for him to air his knowledge about all things to do with the railways.

'The Tin Hares,' said Leo, authoritatively, 'were little motor trains. They only made about forty of them. Sometimes they just ran as a single carriage but they'd often join two or three together if there were a lot of passengers.'

'But why call them "Tin Hares"?' Backhoe persisted.

'I was getting to that. Keep your shirt on. As it happens they were introduced around the same time as they began using a mechanical hare for greyhounds to chase.'

'When was that?' I asked.

'Back in the '20s,' replied Leo. 'The way the rail motors sped along those branch lines reminded people of how the tin hare whipped around on the rail at the greyhound track.

'The first ones they built were just like trucks on wheels – even had gears,' Leo smiled. 'They didn't work very well so they quickly turned them back into trucks. Then they built ones with two engines in, one at each end; they had their radiators on the roof and they were very successful too, particularly on the pioneer lines.'

'What were pioneer lines?' I enquired, as it seemed to be what was expected.

'The pioneer lines,' said Leo, warming to his subject, 'were the branch lines that didn't get a great deal of traffic. They'd lay the rails on very little ballast, sometimes only ashes or even just dirt. Of course, this only worked over flat country, but the lines were cheap and easy to build.'

'Wasn't that a bit dangerous?' asked Backhoe.

'You might have thought that they'd have a lot of derailments but they didn't,' said Leo. 'You see, they put a loco speed limit of fifteen mph on them so they were pretty slow. But the old Tin Hare was less than half the weight of a steam loco and they could really move along those lines. Though they had a steel chassis, they were made of wood with a canvas roof, and because of their light weight, they were ideal for whipping along those pioneer lines and able to go much faster than the old mixed trains. They really cut the running time between towns on branch lines. People loved them.'

'How fast could they go?' asked Backhoe Bill ingenuously.

'They could scoot along at seventy mph,' said Leo. 'But of course they usually wouldn't let them go that fast. The other reason railway people loved them was that you didn't have to steam them up – just start them up and away you'd go. Really easy to stable at night, no ash boxes to clean out. Just fill 'em up with diesel in the morning and that was it.'

'It still takes a bit to start a big diesel, though,' put in Backhoe Bill.

'Yes,' said Leo hastily, before the conversation could turn to backhoes, 'but, if they wouldn't start of a morning, if it was a bit cold for instance, then they could be clutch-started like a car. The driver would turn the ignition on, a steam loco would give them a bit of a push and bingo … you were on your way.'

'Sometimes they just ran as a single carriage.' Crossing the Lachlan at Forbes. DF

'Sounds like they were more reliable than the trains we have today,' mused Backhoe Bill.

'They've been gone for many years now,' said Leo, with a sigh. 'Buses and cars beat them.'

'I remember them too,' I added. 'You used to have to change trains and get one where the electric line stopped.'

'Yes, that's right,' Leo remembered. 'I caught them many times and they were the most sociable of trains to travel on. They were the only trains where you could sit up the front next to the driver and get a driver's eye view of the trip. The driver sat in the front of the carriage and there was a seat either side of him. Blokes on the railway used to call them "the suicide seats".

'While you sat there you could talk to the drivers. Kids loved it and the drivers were mostly pretty good blokes too.'

'I think they had a guard as well, didn't they?' I ventured.

'Yes, every Tin Hare had a guard as well,' Leo agreed, 'and his compartment was in the middle of the carriage with a few fold-down seats in case there was a large crowd on board. The other unusual thing about the old Tin Hares was that half the carriage was first class and the other half was second class.'

'Was there much difference?' asked Backhoe Bill.

Leo was in his element. 'No, the only difference I could tell was that the first-class seats were green and the second class, brown. No one ever seemed to give a stuff about where you sat. The driver could drive from both ends so sometimes the second class was up the front of the train and other times the first-class end was first.'

'Very egalitarian little trains they were,' I put in, remembering my own childhood trips on rail motors. 'Where did you used to catch them, Leo?'

'I've caught them all over the place,' replied Leo, 'but the line that I travelled on most was the one between Wollongong and Moss Vale. They used to run a Tin Hare up the escarpment from Wollongong in

'They had their radiators on the roof and they were very successful, too.'
Tin Hare at Caragabel. DF

the morning and one would come back down in the evening. For some reason it was known among railwaymen as "the Squirt".'

'Strange name for a train,' said Backhoe Bill.

'Lots of trains had strange names back then,' said Leo. He sipped his beer and took up his narrative. 'When the Squirt was coming down that steep grade from Moss Vale, it'd run out of air for its brakes. The guard used to have to put on the handbrake to stop it careering down the line into the Pacific Ocean. I used to help him sometimes.'

'You'd put the brakes on anything, even a good party,' said Henry the Hun, who'd been uncharacteristically quiet for some time.

But nothing could stop Leo now.

'The good thing about that trip was that you could have a drink in the Moss Vale Hotel opposite the railway station before catching the Tin Hare back down the mountain. One time a mate and meself were in there drinking and we couldn't decide whether or not to have another beer.' Leo chuckled to himself, sipped his beer and went on. 'I reckoned we didn't have time to go for another beer and if we had one

Loco 3813 chasing the Tin Hare. DF

more we'd miss the train. My mate said we had plenty of time and we should have one more.'

'It was probably your turn to shout,' commented Henry.

Leo ignored the jibe. 'Anyway, this bloke who was drinking beside us suddenly tapped me on the shoulder and said, "It's all right, you've got plenty of time. You won't miss the train."

'"Oh, really," I said to him. "How would you know?"

'"Well," he says, "I'm the driver of that Tin Hare and there's no way it's going to go until I'm ready. Around here trains don't go without drivers." He turned out to be a real nice bloke, so I bought a few stubbies and as there was no one else on the Squirt we shared them with him and the guard all the way back to Unanderra.'

'You know,' said Henry the Hun, 'my Great Uncle Clarrie used to drive a Tin Hare. He did it for years.'

Leo looked at him suspiciously. Backhoe and I did the same. Henry claimed to have twenty-five great uncles and had used almost all of them in his stories. But we'd never heard of Great Uncle Clarrie.

'What railway line did your Great Uncle Clarrie drive Tin Hares on?' asked Leo.

'He didn't drive 'em on any *line*,' chuckled Henry the Hun. 'He drove the tin hare at the Dapto Dogs for twenty years, and he never once let a greyhound catch it, either.'

'What about you drive yourself over to the bar,' said Leo the Lover. 'It's your shout ...'

# PERHAPS I'M SENTIMENTAL

by *Jim Haynes*

*Perhaps I'm sentimental, but, in my mind, I seem*
*To remember childhood journeys through a veil of smoke and steam.*
*And, down the tunnel of time, I see a past for which I yearn,*
*When a train trip was an adventure, a chance to live and learn.*

*The world passed by those windows, backyards and country scenes,*
*Just like those on the carriage walls and, in my childhood dreams,*
*I was an adventurer, like those fettlers on trikes outback,*
*A battler waiting to jump a freight, a traveller down life's track.*

*How lucky we were to be alive when a train trip meant a ride*
*Behind an engine like a living thing, with its insides all outside.*
*And a platform ticket for a penny was little price to pay*
*For the joy of those reunions, or the sorrow of going away.*

*You don't meet many people in a car or bus or plane,*
*But there was many a friendship made to the rhythm of a train.*
*If you dream of steam and carriages, card games and conversation,*
*Well, perhaps you're sentimental too, and I'll see you at the station.*

'An engine like a living thing, with its insides all outside.' NSW SA

'Through a veil of smoke and steam ... down the tunnel of time.' WCL

# BIBLIOGRAPHY

Lord and Lady Apsley, *The Amateur Settlers*, Hodder & Stoughton, London, 1929

Jeannie Gunn, *We of the Never Never*, Hutchinson, London, 1907

John Gunn, *Along Parallel Lines*, Melbourne University Press, Melbourne, 1989

Edmond La Meslee, *The New Australia*, Heinemann, London, 1973

D.H. Lawrence, *Kangaroo*, Thomas Seltzer, New York, 1923

Andrew Messner, *Train Up!*, Australian Railway Memorial, Werris Creek, NSW, 2003

Henry Handel Richardson, *The Getting of Wisdom*, Heinemann, London, 1910

Steele Rudd, *On an Australian Farm*, NSW Bookstall, Sydney, 1910

Robert Louis Stevenson & Lloyd Osbourne, *The Wrecker*, Cassell & Company, London, 1892

Mark Twain, *Following the Equator*, Harper & Brothers, New York, 1897

# PICTURE CREDITS

| | |
|---|---|
| **ANU NB** | Australian National University Noel Butlin Archives Centre |
| **ARHS NSW RRC** | Australian Railways Historical Society NSW Railway Resource Centre |
| **BCC** | Brisbane City Council |
| **CH** | Chris Holley |
| **DF** | David Field |
| **NSW SA** | New South Wales State Archive |
| **NSW PTU** | New South Wales Public Transport Union |
| **NTL FPPV** | Northern Territory Library Federal Parliamentary Party Visit 1912 Collection |
| **NTL JB** | Northern Territory Library John Blakeman Collection |
| **NTL JM** | Northern Territory Library Jim Mitchell Collection |
| **NTL Misc** | Northern Territory Library Miscellaneous Collection |
| **NTL NTGP** | Northern Territory Library NT Govt Photograph Collection |
| **NTL R** | Northern Territory Library Roderick Collection |
| **RB/EP** | Russell Bright, courtesy of Eveleigh Press |
| **RH** | Russell Hannah |
| **TCL** | Thuringowa City Library |
| **WCL** | Wollongong City Library |
| **WC RTM** | Werris Creek Rail Town Museum |